Contents

About this Book

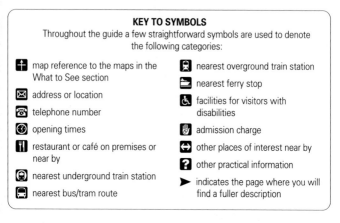

Essential *Portugal* is divided into five sections to cover the most important aspects of your visit to Portugal.

Viewing Portugal pages 5–14
An introduction to Portugal by the author
Portugal's Features
Essence of Portugal
The Shaping of Portugal
Peace and Quiet
Portugal's Famous

Top Ten pages 15–26
The author's choice of the Top Ten places to see in Portugal, each with practical information.

What to See pages 27–90
The four main areas of Portugal, each with its own brief introduction and an alphabetical listing of the main attractions
Practical information
Snippets of 'Did You Know…' information
4 suggested walks
4 suggested tours
2 features

Where To… pages 91–116
Detailed listings of the best places to eat, stay, shop, take the children and be entertained.

Practical Matters pages 117–24
A highly visual section containing essential travel information.

Maps
All map references are to the individual maps found in the What to See section of this guide.
For example, the town of Tavira has the reference ✚ 89E2 – indicating the page on which the map is located and the grid square in which the town is to be found. A list of the maps that have been used in this travel guide can be found in the index.

Prices
Where appropriate, an indication of the cost of an establishment is given by **£** signs:
£££ denotes higher prices, **££** denotes average prices, while **£** denotes lower charges.

Star Ratings
Most of the places described in this book have been given a separate rating:
✪✪✪ Do not miss
✪✪ Highly recommended
✪ Worth seeing

Viewing
Portugal

Martin Symington's Portugal

Islands

Although beyond the scope of this book, the Portuguese state includes two self-governing archipelagos out in the Atlantic Ocean: warm, blooming Madeira and its more barren sister island Porto Santo off the coast of Morocco; and the volcanic mountain tops which are the Azores, poking out of the Atlantic, roughly two thirds of the way across, between Lisbon and New York.

Millions of holidaymakers have visited Portugal over the last thirty years. The great majority of them have been lured to the Algarve by the south coast's sandy coves, manicured golf links, gaily painted fishing boats and lively nightlife in the busy resorts; few are disappointed. Others explore the great cities of Porto and Lisbon, or seek out the swinging resorts of Estoril and Cascais on the Lisbon coast.

The real joy of travelling in Portugal is that it is still one of the least discovered corners of Western Europe. A feeling of isolation still permeates the character of this nation of 10 million souls out on the southwest extremity of the continent. Other than the Algarve, Lisbon area, Porto and a few tourist spots, Portugal still neither gets, nor expects, many visitors. Consequently, there are boundless opportunities for travellers to get close to this beautiful country and its people.

In the lush, green Minho in the far north of the country, many a traveller has been overwhelmed by local hospitality – particularly people who have stayed in private homes under the *Turismo de Habitacão* scheme (► 101).

Portugal offers true wilderness, too, in the remote Penêda-Gerêz and Montesinho national parks, and in the wilds of the Serra da Estrêla, the country's highest mountain range. Southwards, you need only drive a couple of hours from the Algarve's beach resorts to find the cork-forested plains of the Alentejo, sprinkled with dazzling white, Moorish-style villages.

These are the aspects of Portugal which travellers, fired with a spirit of adventure and a dose of curiosity, should try and explore.

Seaweed, a traditional fertiliser, is harvested on the Aveiro Ria, using long-prowed moliceiro *boats*

Portugal's Features

Geography

Portugal lies at the southwest extremity of continental Europe, forming the western edge of the Iberian peninsula. The country's only neighbour is Spain, with whom the River Minho forms a natural border in the north. Eastwards a backbone of craggy mountains divides the old adversaries, while expansive plains stretch down to the sea.

Climate

The Algarve enjoys a Mediterranean-type climate with long hot summers, mild winters and more than 3,000 hours of sunshine a year, although there is always a possibility of rain between September and May.

In the Alentejo, the hinterland of the Beiras and the Alto Douro, summers can be searingly hot. Spring and autumn are cooler, with winters in the mountain regions getting very cold with sub-zero temperatures and snow in the Serra da Estrêla.

Porto and the Minho enjoy a temperate climate, with cooler temperatures year round, and the strong possibility of rain any time between autumn and spring.

Population

The current population is about 10 million, although around 3 million more Portuguese live as migrant workers in France, Germany, the USA, Canada, Venezuela and elsewhere.

Language

The national language is Portuguese. In written form, it appears similar to Spanish, but the sound is much more guttural, making it generally more difficult for foreigners to learn and understand.

Religion

About 99 per cent of the Portuguese population is Roman Catholic. There are small Protestant and Jewish communities.

General Figures

Portugal is roughly rectangular, 560km long from north to south, and 215km wide. Two great rivers, the Douro and the Tejo (Tagus) rise in Spain and flow across the country to their mouths at Porto and Lisbon respectively.

The highest peak in Portugal is Torre in the Serra da Estrêla at 1,993m. A metal post has been added to top the 2,000m mark.

Above: *port vineyards are hewn and blasted out of mountain sides in the wild Douro valley*

Essence of Portugal

Portugal is the last remaining relatively undis-covered country of Western Europe. Those with enough time on their hands to travel from one end to the other will discover a staggering variety of scenery, archi-tecture and ways of life.

They will also find a country whose national character has been shaped by history, geography and centuries of warfare with Spain, Portugal's great Iberian rival. Portugal looks out to sea. Cut off from the rest of Europe, it has always had to do so. This explains why such a small nation became one of the great seafaring peoples of the world.

Today, Portugal is a modern state and a member of the European Union, but the visitor need not dig very deep to find more ancient traditions.

Above: *rustic clothes are gradually giving way to modern garb in rural areas*
Below: *donkey carts are still a feature of tbe Algarve's backwaters*

THE **10** ESSENTIALS

If you only have a short time to visit Portugal, or would like to get a really complete picture of the country, here are the essentials:

• **Walk along the quayside in Lisbon's Belém district**. Admire the great 'Manueline' showpieces of the Jerónimos Monastery and the Belém Tower. You will not fail to sense the spirit of the great Portuguese explorers (➤ 49–56).

• **Go to a** *fado* **house**. The songs you will hear lay Portugal's soul bare, and express the notion of *saudade* – a deep longing for something lost (➤ 114).

• **Stand on Europe's most southwesterly point**, Cabo de São Vicente. It is a suitably dramatic spot for the very corner of a continent. Ships on their way to or from the Mediterranean pass by incredibly close (➤ 18–19).

• **Visit Barcelos market** on a Thursday morning, and barter with the best of them (➤ 38).

• **Sit in the shade of an Alentejo cork tree** or go for a walk through a forest of these beautiful trees whose thick bark is prized all over the world.

• **Go to a village** *festa*. These erupt all over the country, especially in summer, with religious processions, singing, dancing, eating and drinking as fireworks leave a whiff of gun-powder hanging in the air (➤ 116).

• **Walk round the walls of Silves castle**, and feel the wraiths of the Moors, for whom this was once the capital of *Al-Gharb* – 'the Western Land' (➤ 90).

• **Ride on a tram** – in either Lisbon or Porto. Choose one of the clanking, turn-of-the-century ones.

• **Eat a plate of sardines** grilled whole on charcoal. Have them plain, with just some lemon squeezed over them.

• **Drink a glass of port**. Then another. What more needs to be said? Only that you must try also try some chilled *vinho verde*.

Below: *Cabo de São Vicente, Europe's southwesterly extremity*

Below: *trams are a cheap and efficient way of getting around Lisbon*

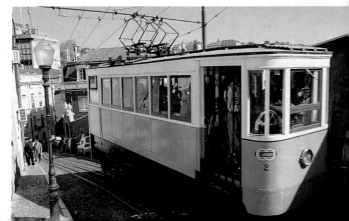

The Shaping of Portugal

2000–1000 BC
Celtic invaders interbreed with the aboriginal tribes of Iberia, to produce the Celt-Iberian civilisation.

About 200 BC
Rome conquers Iberian peninsula, naming much of what is today Portugal *Lusitania*.

About AD 100
Christianity introduced.

About AD 400
Waves of central European tribes invade the Iberian peninsula. Most are driven out by Visigoths, who are allied to the Romans.

711
North African Moors conquer the Iberian peninsula.

Prince Henry the Navigator initiated Portugal's age of exploration

About AD 800
Gradual Christian reconquest begins.

1139
Afonso Henriques wins battle of Campo Ourique against the Moors, and becomes first King of Portugal.

1249
Reconquest of the Algarve from the Moors is completed by King Afonso III.

1385
King Joâo I routs the Castilians at the battle of Aljubarrota.

1386
King Joâo marries Philippa of Lancaster and signs the Treaty of Windsor in alliance with England.

1415
Portugal's great era of discovery and colonial expansion begins with the capture of Ceuta in Morocco.

Left: a statue of Vasco da Gama, another leading figure in the age of discoveries, in Évora

1419–60
Under Prince Henry the Navigator, Portugal discovers Madeira and the Azores and explores the West African coast.

1496
Jews are forced to convert to Christianity or leave Portugal.

1498
Vasco da Gama discovers the sea route to India.

1500
Pedro Cabral is blown off course and accidently discovers Brazil.

1578
King Sebastiâo launches lunatic invasion of Morocco. He and 15,000 men are slaughtered at Al Kasr Al-Kabir.

1580
Philip II of Spain takes advantage of Portugal's weakness and usurps throne.

1587–96
British attack Algarve ports as part of war against Spain.

1640
Following widespread anti-Spanish feeling, Duke of Braganza crowned King João IV, restoring Portugal's independence.

1755
Lisbon and much of southern Portugal, destroyed by earthquake.

1807
Napoleon invades Portugal for failing to support blockade of Britain.

1808–11
The Peninsular War. British forces under Wellington defeat the French and drive them out of Portugal.

1908
King Carlos and his heir assassinated in Lisbon.

1910
Younger son of Carlos, King Manuel II forced into exile. The Republic proclaimed.

1910–26
Country becomes ungovernable, undergoing 45 changes of government.

1916–18
Portugal fights with Allies in World War I.

1926
Army takes over.

1932
Army appoints António Salazar as prime minister. Effectively a dictator, he stays in office until 1968.

1939–45
Portugal remains neutral through World War II.

1960–74
Portugal fights guerilla wars in African colonies of Angola, Mozambique and Guinea-Bissau.

1968
Salazar suffers a stroke (dying two years later) and is replaced as prime minister by Marcelo Caetano.

1974
Right-wing regime overthrown by young left-wing army officers in almost bloodless coup.

1974–6
Series of coups and counter-coups culminating in the establishment of democracy with the election of General António Ramalho Eanes as president. African colonies given independence and descend into vicious civil wars.

1986
Portugal joins the European Community. Mário Soares elected president under a constitution which puts him above party politics. Right-leaning Social Democrat prime

Below: *Sir John Moore leads a retreat to Corunna during the 19th-century Peninsular War*

minister Aníbal Cavaco Silva leads the government.

1995
Socialist government under prime minister António Guterres takes office.

1996
Socialist Jorge Sampaio elected president.

1998
Lisbon set to hold world exposition.

11

Peace & Quiet

Long swathes of dunes and cold, rough seas fringe the Minho coast

West Coast Beaches

To escape the crowds basking on the Algarve's golden sand throughout the summer, head for the west coast. The sea is cooler and rougher, and it can be windy, but there is a genuine sense of isolation. The sandy beaches of Bordeira, Castelejo and Arrifana are the size of athletics stadiums, backed by cliffs sheltering them from the wind. A few serious surfers are attracted here by the great, white Atlantic rollers which break out to sea and rush in noisily. Further north, around Odeceixe, the sand softens to a sandy estuary of wetlands, populated by dazzling white egrets.

Ria Formosa Natural Park

This is a protected area of wetlands, salt-marshes, lagoons and salt pans, around and extending east of Faro, the Algarve's capital. Public access is restricted for conservation reasons but there are several different points around the perimeter where birdwatchers can go to spot egrets, spoonbills and teal.

Berlenga Islands

Lying about 10km offshore and home to huge colonies of seabirds, these are the only islands off the coast of mainland Portugal. They can be visited on day trips from the port of Peniche, near Óbidos (➤ 23) between June and September. Shags, herring gulls and guillemots nest on the cliffs. It is possible to camp overnight or stay at the main island's very basic hostel (☎ 062 750331).

The Aveiro Ria

This great, brackish lagoon (commonly known as the Ria), joined to the sea by a narrow neck of water, spreads its finger-like inlets out across the flat, marshy land, extending 40km in total from Ovar in the north, down to Mira, south of the sea mouth. The rich bird life to be seen here includes herons, egrets, wildfowl and abundant snipe and other waders.

A hump-backed bridge over the Ria north of Aveiro takes the N327 on to the long, narrow spit of sand dunes, pine woods and marshes between the Ria and the sea, leading up to Ovar. There are several places to stop and swim.

Penêda-Gerês National Park

Bordering Spain in the far north of the country, these mountains include some of the wildest, most dramatic scenery Portugal has to offer. This is a gorse and boulder-strewn wilderness splintered by ravines and noisy streams, and fringed by granite peaks where buzzards and kestrels soar. There are waymarked walking trails and campsites within the park.

Montesinho Natural Park

Up in the far, northeast corner of the country, this is Portugal at its most remote. The park begins just north of Bragança, and extends up to the mountains which form a natural border with Spain. This giant hump of wild and exposed upland, dotted with huge, ancient and magnificent chestnut trees, is richer in wildlife than anywhere else in the country. You may see hares leaping through the heather, and birds of prey hovering overhead. The plentiful wild boar are nocturnal and seldom seen; so are the packs of wolves, which can sometimes be heard howling on a winter's night.

Wild Wolves
Packs of wolves roam isolated pockets of Portugal's remotest forests. They can sometimes be heard howling at night in the Serra da Estrela, or in the Montesinho Natural Park, where they cross from Spain in winter. Sightings are rare, but the image of a long-toothed, salivating beast is imprinted on the mind of every Portuguese child.

The marshes and salt pans of the Aveiro Ria spread finger-like across the Beiras landscape

Portugal's Famous

Vasco da Gama

In the history of a nation which shaped the course of world history by the exploits of its explorers, the name of one such explorer stands head and shoulders above all others: Vasco da Gama.

Born in the ocean-side village of Sines on the Alentejo coast in about 1460 (the exact date of his birth remains uncertain), Vasco da Gama grew up looking out to sea with the scent of ozone in his nostrils.

As a young man, the stocky, black-bearded da Gama joined the King's household, trained as a sea pilot and took part in several expeditions along the West African coast, before being selected, in 1497, to lead the greatest quest of all – to discover for good and all, whether or not a sea route to India existed. If it did, untold riches would flow from the trade in spices between Europe and the East.

After a night spent awake and in prayer, Vasco da Gama set sail from Belém on 7 July 1497 with four ships and a crew of 170. He followed the route pioneered by Bartolomeu Dias down to the Cape of Good Hope. On 25 December he came ashore east of the cape, naming this land Natal ('Christmas' in Portuguese), as this province of South Africa is still called today.

Da Gama and his little fleet then became the first Europeans ever to sail up the East African coast. They dropped anchor at Malindi, in present day Kenya, and engaged the services of an Arab pilot, already skilled at navigating the Arabian Sea.

The final leg of the outward voyage took just 26 days. On 18 May 1498 Vasco da Gama reached Calicut on the Malabar coast of western India. The Portuguese were initially regarded with suspicion and their gifts from King Manuel of Portugal were scorned. However, three months later, they set sail for home with a cargo of spices.

The return to Portugal was more hazardous, with storms and scurvy taking heavy tolls. In September 1499, more than two years after he had left, Vasco da Gama sailed up the Tagus and docked at Belém amid scenes of great jubilation. Only two ships had survived the return journey, and of the 170 crew, only 55 came home.

Os Lusíadas

Portugal's greatest literary work, *Os Lusíadas* (The Luciads), by Luis de Camões, is an epic poem triumphantly celebrating Vasco de Gama's discovery of the sea route to India. The beautifully cadenced prose describes the journey, at times seen through the eyes of Greek gods and goddesses in homage to Western civilisation's Greek roots. *Os Lusíadas* is translated into many languages.

Above: *Vasco da Gama, discoverer of the sea route to India*

14

Top Ten

1
Alcobaça

 58B3

20km south of Batalha

Daily 9–7

Buses from Lisbon (2 hours) and Leiria (45 mins)

Tourist Office: Praça 25 de Abril, opposite abbey (☎ 062 42377)

 Few

Apr–Sep, moderate; Oct–Mar, cheap

One of the most beautiful and atmospheric buildings in Portugal and a shrine to a poignant love story.

The Real Abadia de Santa Maria de Alcobaça (the Royal Abbey of St Mary) was built on the orders of King Afonso I to fulfil a promise he had made to God before a victory over the Moors at Santarem. It was given to the Cistercian order and became immensely rich and powerful, in the finest traditions of medieval monasticism. The monks remained at Alcobaça until the Abbey's confiscation during repression of religious orders in the 19th century. Today, the monastery still dominates this small agricultural town surrounded by fruit-growing estates and vineyards.

The church, the largest in Portugal, is gloriously spacious and built in a refreshingly simple style, as are the 14th-century cloisters where a calming aura lingers, especially if you are able to wander round in silence. More worldly are the gigantic kitchens and monastic cooking utensils.

But it is the tombs of Dom Pedro and Inês de Castro which attract the greatest attention. The pair are Portuguese history's irrepressible lovers – Pedro was a prince and Inês the daughter of a nobleman from Galicia with whom he had fallen in love. His father, King Afonso, had her murdered to avoid allowing the Galicians influence in Portuguese affairs. Pedro rebelled against his father and two years later became king, holding the memory of Inês dear for the rest of his life. Both were buried at Alcobaça in tombs with intricate carvings telling their story; the tombs are toe-to-toe so that the first thing they see on Judgement Day will be each other.

Famous lovers Pedro and Inês are entombed toe to toe, so that the first thing they see in resurrection will be each other

4

Monsaraz

  28B2

 Southeast of Évora, 7km off the N256

Restaurants and cafés, including Solar de Monsaraz (££)

Daily bus service from Évora (45 mins)

Tourist Office: Largo Nuno Álvares (☎ 066 55136)

Few

One of Portugal's most spectacular fortified hilltop villages, nestling within impregnable stone walls.

Monsaraz is one of a long chain of fortified villages near Portugal's eastern border with Spain, built for their commanding positions; Romans, Visigoths and Moors all had settlements here, before the Christian re-conquest. The village itself has a sleepy, medieval mien – the main street is too narrow for a car; park outside the main gate.

The present castle and formidable ramparts are 14th-century, built by King Dinis. In front of the pentagonal castle keep is a square where bullfights are held on feast days with villagers cheering from the walls.

The view from the parapet is stunning: the plains of the Alentejo stretch out endlessly towards the coast, whose outline just becomes visible on the horizon when the air is exceptionally clear. The rocky, meandering Guadiana river, to the east, provides a dramatic contrast, while Spain extends beyond like a crumpled rug.

Monsaraz is one of the most quintessential of Portuguese villages

There are several points of interest on Rua Direita, the cobbled main street, which is lined with houses embla-zoned with the coats of arms of wealthy 16th–17th-century families. The Paços do Concelho Tribunal building has a 15th-century fresco depicting a judge being tempted by an impish, bride-offering devil while simultaneously being drawn into the outstretched arms and majestic justice of Christ.

The Igreja Matriz parish church is also worth a look.

5

Mosteiro dos Jerónimos
(Jerónimos Monastery)

*The crowning glory of Manueline architecture,
built on riches which followed the discovery
of trade routes to the east.*

Jerónimos is the classic example of Manueline architecture, the home-grown style through which a tiny nation
proclaimed its greatness to the world. The monastery is
built on the site of the Santa Maria hermitage, which
Prince Henry the Navigator founded in 1460, the year of
his death. This was hugely embellished by Dom Manuel in
the following century to commemorate Vasco da Gama's
discovery of the sea route to India in 1498.

Accordingly, the buildings are adorned with ocean-going
and oriental motifs such as seahorses, elephants, ropes
and armillary spheres, all elaborately carved in stone. The
southern façade, looking out over the Tagus estuary, is
sensationally grand. A bearded statue of Prince Henry
stands at the south portal. Dom Manuel and his wife Dona
Maria preside over the west portal, in the company of the
four evangelists.

Most breathtaking of all is
the cavernous interior; six great
supporting columns are styled
as colossal palm trees with
fanned ribbed vaulting as their
fronds. Inside are the tombs and
stone effigies of several kings
supported by elephants, and of
two of Portugal's greatest
heroes – Vasco da Gama himself, and Luis de Camões,
who told the story of his discoveries in the epic poem *Os
Lusíadas* (▶ 14).

The monastery was seriously
damaged in the 1755 earthquake but many of the splendid
features survived unscathed,
including the elaborate and
majestic west portal. The
cloisters are on two storeys,
carved with fantastic and surreal
animals and distorted human
figures secreted among intricate
vegetation.

Right: *Manueline buildings – the
status symbols of a superpower*

✚	Off map 52A1
✉	Belém, Lisbon
🕐	Tue–Sun 10–5
🚌	Buses from the Baixa district; tram 15
🚉	On the Avenida de Brasília
⛴	Ferry to Trafaria, across the Tagus
♿	Few
✋	Church free; Cloisters cheap Oct–May; moderate Jun–Sep

21

6
Museu Calouste Gulbenkian

*An astounding collection of artistic riches
from across the centuries,
bequeathed by the oil magnate.*

 Off map 52C4

 Avenida da Berna 45, Lisbon

 Oct–May Tue–Sun 10–5; Jun–Sep Tue, Thu, Fri and Sun 10–5, Wed and Sat 2–7:30, closed Mon and public holidays

Café-bar (££)

Metro S Sebastião Palhavã

Bus 16, 26, 31, 46, 56

 Good

Tue–Mon cheap, Sun free

*A 14th-century mosque
lamp is one of thousands
of treasures in the
Gulbenkian collection*

Calouste Gulbenkian was an Armenian oil magnate who, shortly after the turn of the century, acquired a five per cent share in the oil fields of Iraq. As the 20th century progressed, man's dependence on the internal combustion engine burgeoned and Gulbenkian grew phenomenally wealthy. In 1942 he adopted Portugal, neutral during World War II, as his homeland.

He died in Lisbon in 1955, bequeathing his vast array of treasures and huge fortune to the establishment of a foundation for 'charitable, artistic, educational and scientific' purposes. The foundation's assets now make it the largest charity in Europe.

The museum, set in beautiful green gardens, was opened by the foundation in 1969, and includes seven principal collections: Egyptian art; Graeco-Roman art; Middle Eastern and Islamic art; Oriental art; a collection of French ivories; painting and sculpture (including works by Rembrandt, Rubens, Gainsborough and Manet, and a superb marble statue of Diana by Houbon) and furniture and furnishings.

The museum also houses smaller, rare collections, such as snuff boxes, French bookbindings, European ceramics, art nouveau jewellery and gold and silver work.

Across the gardens from the main museum is the Centro de Arte Moderna (Modern Art Centre), a new extension opened in 1983. The centre houses both permanent and temporary exhibitions, with a strong emphasis on 20th-century Portuguese artists such as Almada Negreiros, who was the founder of the school of Portuguese Modernism. There is also some excellent modern sculpture on display in the centre, including work by Henry Moore.

The North

The north is the cradle of the nation, where the Kingdom of Portugal was proclaimed in the 12th century. The centre of power shifted south many centuries ago, though the North remains richly historic. Towns such as Guimarães and Coimbra have both, for short periods, been the national capital.

Scenically the region is extremely diverse, from the lush and fertile Minho, north of Porto, described as the Costa Verde (Green Coast), to the austere mountains of the Serra da Estrêla and the grape-growing Douro valley. In between are the somnolent marches and salt pans of the Aveiro lagoon.

The quintessential Portuguese conservatism is more evident in the north – even in Porto, the country's second city – than in the south. For this reason, the people of the north are sometimes accused by their compatriots of backwardness.

*'Be sometimes to your country true,
Have once the public good in view.
Bravely despise Champagne at Court,
And choose to dine at home with Port.'*

JONATHAN SWIFT (1726)

Porto (Oporto)

Portugal's second largest city has a history going back some 4,000 years, making it one of the oldest towns in Europe. As a booming industrial centre some find it ugly. Others are quick to discover the charms of the old town and the vinous treats of Vila Nova de Gaia's port lodges (▶ 26).

For most visitors Porto's heart is in its old town, on the north bank of the river. The area is coloured by dense clusters of tall, dilapidated, red-tiled houses thrown haphazardly together in what looks like an oversized village spilling down from the city centre to the Ribeira district on the River Douro quay side.

Alleys and walkways, some of them tortuously steep, wind through this labyrinth of homes and artisans' workshops; women in voluminous skirts sell fruit,

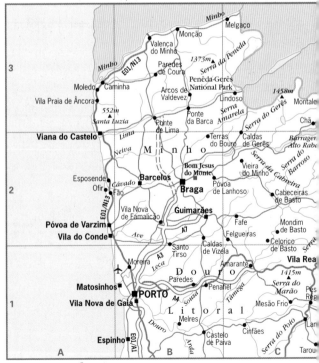

vegetables and sardines, and washing lines overhead flap with white sheets and brightly coloured clothing. Far from being a sanitised old town, as is found in so many European cities, this is a real living quarter, buzzing with activity.

Porto's ancient, rickety trams are a fun way to get around. Hop on one anywhere along the Douro quayside, and it will take you along the river to its mouth. However, most sightseeing can be done within a fairly short walk of the city centre, though you do need stamina for the steep gradients.

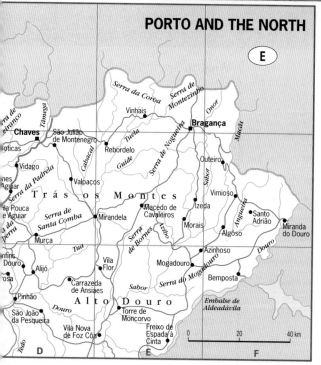

PORTO AND THE NORTH

E

Chaves
São Julião de Montenegro
Vinhais
Bragança
Onor
Maças
Serra da Coroa
Serra de Montezinho
Tâmega
oticas
Vidago
Rebordelo
Tuela
Guide
Outeiro
Serra de Nogueira
Sabor
Serra da Padrela
Cabaçal
nes
Aguiar
Valpaços
Trás os Montes
Vimioso
Anguena
ila Pouca
e Aguiar
Serra de Santa Comba
Mirandela
Macedo de Cavaleiros
Izeda
Morais
Santo Adrião
Miranda do Douro
da
erra
Murça
Serra de Bornes
Azibo
Algóso
nfins
Douro
Alijó
Tua
Vila Flor
Mogadouro
Azinhoso
Douro
osa
Carrazeda de Ansiães
Sabor
Serra do Mogadouro
Bemposta
Pinhão
Alto Douro
Torre de Moncorvo
Embalse de Aldeadávila
São João da Pesqueira
Douro
Freixo de Espada à Cinta
Vila Nova de Foz Côa
0   20   40 km
Têdo

D   E   F

What to See in Porto

IGREJA DE SÃO FRANCISCO CHURCH
(CHURCH OF ST FRANCIS) ✪✪

One of the most amazing churches in Portugal, and to most tastes infinitely more beautiful than the Sé. Dazzling and intricate gilt work extends from ceiling to floor; it is said that there are over 400kg of pure gold inside.

MUSEU DE SOARES DOS REIS ✪

Porto's principal museum occupies an 18th-century neo-classical home of the powerful Morães e Castro family, which later served as the headquarters of the Napoleonic forces during the Peninsular War. It is said that Wellington and his officers, having defeated the French and ousted Marshall Soult in 1809, ate their dinner here.

The spectacle was probably rather more arresting than this somewhat down-at-heel museum, which houses displays of 19th-and early 20th-century Portuguese art. There are several items worth seeing, however, including the sculptures of Soares dos Reis, the 19th-century sculptor after whom the museum is named; paintings by Vasco Fernandes (▶ 47); and collections of Portuguese painted glass and porcelain. Exotica from outside Portugal includes tortoiseshell and silver boxes from Goa, some

🕂 33B1
✉ Rua Infante D Henrique
🕓 Tue–Sat 9–12, 2–5 (Jul–Aug 9–5)
♿ None
▥ Moderate

🕂 33A2
✉ Rua de Dom Manuel II
☎ 02 200 7110
🕓 Tue–Sun 10–12, 2–5. Closed Mon and public holidays
♿ Few
▥ Free Sundays, moderate Tue–Sat
❓ Special exhibitions

fine German altar chalices, and English furniture.

PALÁCIO DA BOLSA ✪✪✪

The fine 19th-century granite and marble palace once housed the city's parliament and judiciary as well as the stock exchange. A tour of the palace, compulsorily with a guide, is from echoing hall to sumptuous salon; it includes numerous exhibits illustrating the history of Porto, and makes an excellent introduction to the city. The star attraction of the palace is the amazing Arab Room, decorated in brilliant Moorish style with gilding, stained-glass windows, painted stucco and a pastiche of the Alhambra in Granada, Spain.

➕ 33B1
✉ Praça do Infante D Henrique
🕐 Mon–Sun 9–12:40, 2–5:40
🍴 Plentiful restaurants and cafés in the nearby Ribeira
♿ Few
💰 Moderate

Left: *the double-decker Dom Luis I bridge spans the Douro between Porto and Vila Nova de Gaia*

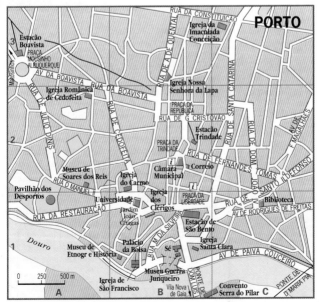

PORTO

Estação Boavista
PRAÇA MOUSINHO ALBUQUERQUE
AV DA BOAVISTA
RUA DA BOAVISTA
Igreja Românica de Cedofeita
Igreja da Imaculada Conceição
RUA DA CONSTITUIÇÃO
RUA DE A DE QUENTAL
Igreja Nossa Senhora da Lapa
PRAÇA DA REPÚBLICA
RUA DE G CRISTOVÃO
Estação Trindade
PRAÇA DA TRINDADE
RUA DE JÚLIO DINIS
RUA DE CEDOFEITA
RUA DE SANTA CATARINA
RUA DE DOM TOMAS
AV DE MAGALHÃES
Museu de Soares dos Reis
RUA D MANUEL II
Igreja do Carmo
Câmara Municipal
RUA DE FERNANDES TOMÁS
Correio
Pavilhão dos Desportos
Universidade
Igreja dos Clérigos
PRAÇA DA LIBERDADE
RUA DE SANTO ILDEFONSO
RUA DA RESTAURAÇÃO
Jardim João Chagas
Estação de São Bento
AV DE RODRIGUES DE FREITAS
Biblioteca
Douro
Museu de Etnogr e História
Palácio da Bolsa
RUA DA SILVEIRA
Sé
Igreja Santa Clara
AV DE PAIVA COUCEIRO
0 250 500 m
Igreja de São Francisco
Museu Guerra Junqueiro
Vila Nova de Gaia
PONTE DE DOM LUIS I
Convento Serra do Pilar
PONTE DE D MARIA PIA
A
B
C

The Cathedral's high altar, typical of the ornate baroque which can be found in churches throughout Portugal

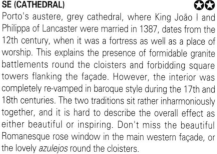

33B1
Terreiro da Sé
Daily 9–12, 2:30–5:30
Many nearby cafés
Few
Church free; cloisters cheap
Occasional classical concerts

SÉ (CATHEDRAL) ⭐⭐

Porto's austere, grey cathedral, where King João I and Philippa of Lancaster were married in 1387, dates from the 12th century, when it was a fortress as well as a place of worship. This explains the presence of formidable granite battlements round the cloisters and forbidding square towers flanking the façade. However, the interior was completely re-vamped in baroque style during the 17th and 18th centuries. The two traditions sit rather inharmoniously together, and it is hard to describe the overall effect as either beautiful or inspiring. Don't miss the beautiful Romanesque rose window in the main western façade, or the lovely *azulejos* round the cloisters.

33B1
Rua dos Clérigos
200 1729
Daily 10–12, 2–5. Church closed Wed
None
Cheap

TORRE DOS CLÉRIGOS ⭐

This soaring, rocket-like 75m-high granite tower of the Igreja dos Clérigos, has been a main feature of the Porto skyline since the building was completed in 1749. The exhausting climb to the top is up a spiral staircase of 225 worn steps, and is rewarded by fabulous views over the city, or severe vertigo, or both.

VILA NOVA DE GAIA (► 26, TOP TEN)

Porto Walk

Starting at Estaçao de São Bento

Porto's central railway station is built on the foundations of Ave Maria convent, of which a few vestiges remain. Whether you are travelling by train or not, the station is worth visiting to see its fabulous collection of giant *azulejo* murals, depicting great events in the city's history.

Walk up the Avenida de Afonso Henriques to the Sé (Cathedral ➤ 34).

The main doors of the Sé give on to a pedestrianised square from where a stone staircase leads down into the warren of alleys which is Porto's old town. Twist down through this labyrinth, to emerge on Rua Infante Dom Henrique.

Turn right along Rua Infante Dom Henrique, till you reach the Praça do Infante Dom Henriques.

Visit the Palácio da Bolsa (➤ 33) and the adjacent Igreja São Francisco (➤ 32)

Walk back along Rua Infante Dom Henrique to the Feitoria Inglesa.

This fine 18th-century town house is a 'factory' in the old-fashioned sense of a meeting place of 'factors' or merchants rather than a manufactory. It is now the headquarters of the British Association of Port Shippers, and the interior can only be visited by invitation from a member.

Turn right and follow the Rua de São João down to the Praça da Ribeira square, leading on to the Cais da Ribeira.

The Cais da Ribeira are at the heart of the tourist area with restaurants, cafés, handicraft shops and an open air market. The vista across the river to Vila Nova da Gaia, with the double-decker Dom Luis I bridge looming large a little way upstream, is spectacular.

Follow the quay up to the bridge, continuing for a few metres along Avenida Gustave Eiffel, then climb the long stone staircase up to the Avenida de Vimara Peres, emerging by the Dom Luis Bridge at its upper level.

Distance
3km

Time
2–5 hours, depending on length of visits

Start point
São Bento Station
🚇 33B1

End point
Upper level, Dom Luis Bridge
🚇 33B1

Lunch
Taverna do Bebóbos (££)
✉ Cais da Ribeira 24
☎ 02 313565

The Ribeira district is both a focus for tourism and a real living quarter

What to See in the North

AMARANTE ⊗⊗

 30C1

✉ 56km east of Porto

❓ Colourful festival on first weekend Jun

São Gonçalo Church

🕐 Cloisters Tue–Sun 10–12, 2–5

♿ Few 🎫 Free

Amarante is an enchanting little town which sits beside the Tâmega river, spanned by the photogenic 18th-century São Gonzalo bridge of honey-coloured granite. Terraces and verandahs overlook the willow-lined water where anglers cast for trout. A tiled cupola rises above the mellow stone of the 16th-century São Gonçalo convent. Inside is the tomb of São Gonçalo himself; votive offerings are left in the Chapel of Miracles.

The restaurant Zé da Calçada (➤ 92) is the best place to sit and admire the views over the river, and also to try one of Portugal's rarer culinary delicacies – the town's famous *bolos de São Gonzalo* (cakes).

Aveiro

 36A3

✉ 52km south of Porto

ℹ Tourist Office: Rua João Mendonça 8 (☎ 034 236 80)

❓ Aveiro holds a major festival at the end of August (dates variable), with *moliceiro* boat races

Votive offerings are left at the tomb of São Gonzalo

THE BEIRAS

PORTO
Vila Nova de Gaia
Penafiel
Cinfães
Castelo de Paiva
Espinho
Feira
São João de Madeira
Arouca
Furadouro
Vale de Cambra
Serra da Arr
Ovar
Torreira
Estarreja
Sever do Vouga
São Pe da
Murtosa
Oliveira de Frades
Vou
Ria d'Aveiro
Aveiro
Albergaria-a-velha
Ílhavo
Águeda
Vagos
Oliveira de Bairro
Serra do Caramulo
Caramu
Praia de Mira
Anadia
1075m
Tondela
Oliv do Co
Mira
Mealhada
Luso
Santa
Cantanhede
Serra do Buçaco
Comba Dão
Tocha
Beira
Lorvão
Tábua
Quiaios
Montemor-o-Velho
Coimbra
Vila Nova de Poiares
Arg
Cabo Mondego
Mondego
Figueira da Foz
Condeixa-a-Nova
Góis
Ce
Lavos
Soure
Miranda do Corvo
Lousã
Ruínas de Conímbriga
Penela
Serra da Lousã
Louriçal
Litoral
Castanheira de Pêra
Pampilho de Se
Pombal
Vieira de Leiria
Lis
Monte Real
Ansião
Figueiró dos Vinhos
Serr
São Pedro de Muel
Marinha Grande
Alvaiázere
Serta
Leiria
Nabão
Ferreira do Zêzere
Proen a-N
Batalha
Vila Nova de Ourém
Vila de Re
Nazaré
Barragem do Castelo de Bode
Alcobaça
Fátima
Tomar
A
B

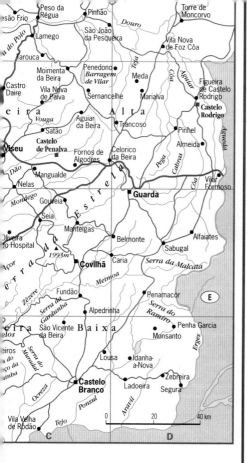

Above: *the tiled façade of a typical Aveiro house*

The Festa das Cruces in Barcelos is one of many festivals that erupt across the Minho in summer

🔲 30B2
✉ 52km northeast of Porto
ℹ Tourist Office: Avenida da Liberdade 1 (☎ 053 225 50)

Sacred Art Museum
🕐 Daily 8:30–6:30
👜 Cheap

unsuspecting; huge piles of fruit and vegetables; cassettes whose vendors try to blast each other out of contention with tinny decks running on car batteries; and clothes ranging from rustic berets to real leather bomber jackets.

The town is worth a brief stop on non-market days to see the enormous square centred by a beautiful fountain.

BRAGA ⭐⭐
Braga is sometimes known as the 'Portuguese Rome'. The town is the religious capital of Portugal. At times during Portuguese history, the Church has wielded more power than the monarchy or government with Braga at the centre of this influence. Since the revolution of 1974 the ecclesiastic and political establishments have had less to do with each other, but Portugal is still a strongly spiritual nation and Braga's Holy Week celebrations in particular

(▶ 116) are a striking testament to the depth of religious feeling here.

There are 80 churches in this town, of which only the Sé (Cathedral) is unmissable. The foundations are 12th-century, with the main west door and the whole southern portal the most obvious visible survivors of the original Romanesque buildings. There are Gothic, Renaissance, baroque and Manueline amongst an extraordinary diversity of styles which somehow come together into a harmonious whole. Most striking is a pair of ornate gilt 18th-century organs adorned with cherubs, dolphins and mermaids. In the Capela de São Pedro (St Peter's Chapel) are some outstanding *azulejos* by the master tile artist António Oliveira Bernardes; also not to be missed is a beautiful fresco of the Virgin in the Gothic Capela de São Geraldo (St Gerald's Chapel) and the Capela dos Reis (Chapel of the Kings) containing the tombs of Dom Henriques and Dona Teresa, whose son, Dom Afonso Henriques, became the first king of Portugal.

Braga's Cathedral interior is an extraordinary hotch-potch of styles

The pick of Braga's other sites are the Capela dos Coimbras (Coimbras Chapel) on Rua do Soto with its flamboyant Manueline tower and, inside, *azulejos* depicting the story of Adam and Eve; the splendid 17th-century baroque Igreja Santa Cruz (Holy Cross Church) on Rua do Anjo; and the extensive Antigo Paço Espiscopal (former Archbishop's Palace) with its peaceful, well-tended Santa Barbara gardens and Largo do Paco courtyard.

Three kilometres outside Braga is an ornate baroque terraced staircase of more than 1,000 steps leading up to the Bom Jesus sanctuary.

Driving Tour of The Douro Valley

Distance
About 330km

Time
Ten hours, including stops

Start point
Low Level, Dom Luis I Bridge, Porto
🚩 33B1

End point
Porto city centre
🚩 33B1

Lunch
Pousada Barão de Forrester (£££)
✉ Alijó

From the lower level of the Dom Luis bridge, meander up the north bank of the river, passing two dams, before arriving at Peso da Régua.

Régua (as it is signposted, and always known) is one of the main port-producing cities, although it offers little to see or do. Better to continue on through the increasingly wild and spectacular scenery.

Cross the road bridge to the south bank of the Douro. From here, a beautiful route follows the river, which is turned into a long, serpentine lake by a huge hydro-electric dam. An iron bridge crosses the river at Pinhão.

Pinhão is a small town at the heart of the port-producing country. The red-tiled roofs of long, barrel warehouses are, as in Vila Nova de Gaia, whitewashed with the familiar names of the great port-shipping companies. The town itself, however, has little to detain the visitor, other than some beautiful *azulejo* tiles on the station platform, depicting traditional Douro rural life.

Another spectacular road twists up the valley of the Pinhão tributary, through dramatic, rocky scenery with mountainsides carved into terraces of vineyards, olive groves and citrus orchards which have been hewn and blasted out of the rock. This road leads up to the small town of Alijó. From here, take the road to Populo, to join the main IP4 Porto/Braganza highway. Pull off the IP4 at the Vila Real signpost, and follow signposts to Sabrosa and Solar de Mateus, which is 3km south of the town.

Hydro-electric dams have transformed the Douro into a series of long, anguine lakes

Solar De Mateus is a splendid, 18th-century palace famous the world over for gracing the label of every bottle of Mateus Rosé sold. There is no other particular connection between between the palace and the wine, so don't expect a tasting. A tour of the treasure-filled palace and beautiful grounds, however, is a treat.

Turn off the IP4 again at the Amarante signpost, to explore this beautiful town (➤ 36). Re-join the IP4 to return to central Porto. There is a toll to pay shortly before you reach the city.

BRAGANÇA (BRAGANZA) ✪✪

Up in the extreme northeast of the country and cut off from the rest of Portugal by three mountain ranges, Bragança stands isolated. Yet behind this remoteness is a city with an illustrious past: it has been fought over from prehistoric times through to the 19th-century Peninsular War, with sieges, battles and invasions turning on control of the walled citadel and its massive grey stone ramparts. The dukedom of Bragança became the royal house of Portugal, and supplied England with a queen, when Charles II married Catherine of Bragança.

There are bustling fruit, vegetable and grain markets distracting attention from the stately churches and fading, grandiose buildings of another era. Steep cobbled lanes lead up to the gates of the citadel and castle walls, within which everyday life goes on around the soaring Gothic keep. Washing hangs drying outside cottages with red-tiled roofs, haphazardly thrown together. Children play and chickens scratch about the vegetable plots and rubbish heaps, creating an almost medieval atmosphere.

Bragança is dominated by its forbidding and seemingly impenetrable **castle.** A tall keep is surrounded by crenellated turrets, with only narrow slits letting in any light. Fittingly, it houses a **Military Museum** charting the history of Portugal at war, with emphasis on the African colonies. From a platform at the top of the keep, there are wonderful views over the town and mountains.

✚ 31E3
✉ 253km northeast of Porto
ℹ Tourist Office: Avenida Cidade de Zamora (☎ 073 22273)
🍴 Many cafés and restaurants in the lower town

Castle and Military Museum
🕐 Fri–Wed 9–12, 2–5. Closed Thu and public holidays
♿ None
💰 Cheap

Above: the forbidding citadel at Bragança has been fortified since prehistoric times

Did you know ?

Catherine of Bragança married English King Charles II. Her dowry included the Portuguese trading post of Bombay, and she introduced to England the custom of taking afternoon tea.

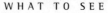

➕ 36B2

✉ 150km northeast of Lisbon

ℹ Tourist Office: Largo da Portagem (☎ 039 23886)

University buildings

🕐 Mon–Sat 9:30–12, 2–5; library 9:30–12, 2–5. Closed Sun and public holidays

Monastery of the Holy Cross

✉ Praça 8 de Maio

🕐 Daily 7:30–12:30, 2–6:30

Conimbriga ruins

✉ 17km south of Coimbra, off the N1

🕐 Daily 9–1, 2–8. Museum 10–1, 2–6

COIMBRA ✪✪✪

Set on a steep hill rising from the north bank of the River Mondego, Coimbra is one of the oldest university towns in Europe. It was also the capital of Portugal in the 12th and 13th centuries, after Guimarães and before Lisbon. Curiously, however, this concentration of historic buildings, romantically set on a hill overlooking the river, makes few concessions to tourism. The atmosphere varies between lively and youthful in term time, and stuffy and museum-like during vacations.

The **Velha Universidade (Old University)** of Coimbra was founded in 1290. Up at the highest point of the city is the institution's main courtyard, enclosed by a great ceremonial hall with a superb, 17th-century painted ceiling; the gloriously flamboyant, Manueline São Miguel chapel; and a small Museum of Sacred Art. The most splendid building in Coimbra, however, is the university library, which is composed of three glittering 18th-century baroque rooms with vast expanses of gilded wood. These have many oriental features, reflecting the Age of Discoveries.

The Sé Velha (the Old Cathedral) is a beautiful Romanesque church with many more recent features, begun in the late 12th century after Coimbra had become capital of the new Kingdom of Portugal. There is a beautiful altarpiece and some fine Renaissance side chapels, but

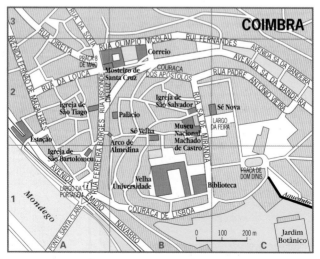

somehow it is the deeply moving ambience of the cathedral which is the true attraction.

Down in the 'new' town is Coimbra's other great architectural jewel, the **Mosteiro da Santa Cruz (Monastery of the Holy Cross)**. Like the cathedral, it was founded in the 12th century by Afonso Henriques, first king of Portugal, since when it has been liberally endowed with embellishments. The most interesting features are the ornate, carved stone pulpit in the centre of the church; the Manueline choir, where the voyages of Vasco da Gama are depicted in gilt wood carvings; and the sacristy where there is a collection of Renaissance art including a number of works by Grão Vasco (► 47).

Seventeen kilometres south of Coimbra, is **Conimbriga**, the largest Roman archaeological site in Portugal. Disappointingly, less than a quarter of the site has been excavated, but it is worth visiting to see the superb mosaic floors that survive.

Above: *Coimbra's glittering university library*
Right: *the 13th-century university, one of the oldest in Europe*

36A2
42km west of Coimbra
Tourist Office: Rua 25 de
Abril (☎ 033 22610)

30B2
49km northeast of Porto
and 22km southeast of
Braga
Tourist Offices: Avenida
Resistência ao Fascismo
83 (☎ 053 412450) and
Praça de Santiago
(☎ 053 515123)

Castle
Tue–Sun 9–5:30. Tower
9–12:30, 2:30–5:30

Paço dos Duques
☎ 053 412273
Daily 10–5:30
None
Oct–May cheap; Jun–Sep
moderate

FIGUEIRA DA FOZ ✪

Figueira da Foz is a fishing port and small beach holiday resort at the mouth of the River Mondego. The chief attraction is the enormous beach, ½km wide; the great Atlantic breakers are popular with surfers, although the rough sea can disappoint families who come hoping to swim. The town has several modern holiday hotels, discos, a casino and tennis courts.

GUIMARÃES ✪✪

In 1139 Afonso Henriques was declared the first king of Portugal, and made Guimarães his capital. Although the centre of power soon shifted south – first to Coimbra and later to Lisbon – Guimarães still has a historic kernel, reached beyond the sprawl of textile and shoe factories which make it an important and prosperous industrial centre.

The ruined 10th-century **castle** stands rather dramatically on a rocky hill in the middle of town. There are seven great towers surrounding the keep, but otherwise little to see other than the great views over Guimarães and the surrounding countryside from the ramparts, which can be easily climbed.

The **Paço dos Duques (Palace of the Dukes of Braganza)** is the principal monument and museum to Guimarães's status as the cradle of the Portuguese nation. A fine, bronze statue of Afonso Henriques stands outside, guarding the four sturdy buildings with massive corner towers, built by Dom Afonso, the first Duke of Bragança. Inside, the unmissable rooms are the banqueting hall with its splendid wooden ceiling, and a fine collection of Persian carpets and Flemish tapestries.

LUSO

The still, fresh mineral water of the famous Luso spa is favoured all over Portugal. It has a high level of radio-activity, which may sound alarming but is, apparently, beneficial. Certainly, many Portuguese regard the waters of Luso as a panacea; liver complaints in particular are reported to be eased at the very mention of a drop of Luso water. The Buçaco Palace Hotel (▶ 100) once described itself in a brochure as 'the shadiest hotel in Portugal'. This was actually a reference to the hotel's beautiful 100ha walled forest of oak, cork, pine and rare imported exotic trees (which do indeed throw a deep shade) with walkways and streams.

SERRA DO CARAMULO

Caramulo is the main town in the Serra do Caramulo, a range of rolling inland mountains little visited by foreign tourists, but an excellent stop for motorists taking a hinterland route between north and south. The town of Caramulo itself is on the edge of the Cambarinho Natural Park, in which rare forms of oleander are conserved, amid vineyards and cattle pasture. The town has a small pousada (▶ 103) and two unlikely museums – one housing a collection of vintage cars, the other 'Ancient and Modern Art' including works by Dali and Picasso.

SERRA DA ESTRÊLA (▶ 24, TOP TEN)

36B2

✉ 25km northeast of Coimbra

ℹ Tourist Office: Rua Emídio Navarro (☎ 031 939133)

Opposite: *Figueira da Foz attracts wind-surfers and board-surfers alike*

36B3

✉ Caramulo is 40km southwest of Viseu

Museu de Arte
☎ 032 861270
🕐 Open daily 10–1 and 2–6
💰 Expensive

Below: *Caramulo boasts Portugal's finest collection of vintage cars*

✚ 30B3

✉ 52km north of Viana do Castelo and 108km north of Porto

🕐 Unrestricted access to the walls

ℹ Tourist Office: Avenida de Espanha (☎ 051 23374)

VALENÇA DO MINHO ★★

Looking across the Minho towards Tuy, its Spanish counterpart, the border town of Valença do Minho has for centuries been on Portugal's front line of defence. Two massive sets of ramparts protect the old town which is entered via a drawbridge; inside are narrow cobbled streets and a lively atmosphere with large numbers of shops, patronised by Spaniards who have crossed the frontier to sniff out the best bargains. There are great views across to Spain from the walls, which can be walked around, and from the *pousada* (▶ 103) set into the ramparts. The new town, at the bottom of the hill outside the walls, has little of interest.

✚ 30A2

✉ 56km north of Porto

ℹ Tourist Office: Rua do Hospital Velho (☎ 058 822620)

❓ Viana stages northern Portugal's greatest *romaria* and *festa*, Nossa Senhora da Agonía, over the weekend nearest to 15 August

VIANA DO CASTELO ★★★

This attractive fishing port, and venue for the greatest *festa* in the north of Portugal each August, stands on the north bank of the Lima estuary, dominated by the lusciously wooded Santa Luzia mountain. The beautiful Praça da República is surrounded by fine houses decorated with Manueline embellishments dating from the 16th and 17th centuries, when the town became prosperous on trade and fishing for *bacalhau* (dried salt cod) from the Grand Banks of Newfoundland, and exporting wine to Britain.

Viana is a delightful town to wander around and has a strong folkloric tradition; on Sundays and saints' days, people are frequently to be seen on the streets wearing traditional regional dress – the women in long embroidered skirts and veils, the men in bright waistcoats and black, broad-brimmed hats.

A narrow 4km road winds up to the basilica and hotel on Monte de Santa Luzia, from where the views over the north of Portugal are sensational. On a clear day the coastline can be traced from the Minho and Spain beyond, most of the way down to Porto.

Above: *sweeping views over Viana do Castelo and the Minho coast from the basilica of Santa Luzia*

46

VISEU ⭐⭐

Viseu is a solemn town of dignified airs at the heart of Dão wine-producing country. Its history is centred on Vasco Fernandes (1480–1543), later styled Grão Vasco – the 'Great Vasco' – founder of the Viseu school of painting. As he was one of the most eminent painters in Portuguese history, and the one principally responsible for introducing the Renaissance to the country, his adopted home town, Viseu, is naturally proud of him. So there is a Grão Vasco museum, a Grão Vasco hotel, and Grão Vasco wine – one of the most famous brands of Dão.

The **Grão Vasco Museum** is housed in the Bishop's Palace opposite the Cathedral. Many of Grão Vasco's most famous works are exhibited, including his interpretations of St Peter and St Sebastian. The museum also contains work by Gaspar Vaz, another Portuguese master, and some beautiful 16th-century *azulejos*.

The twin-towered Cathedral was built in a hotch-potch of different styles, between the 13th and 18th-centuries, and is worth seeing. Most remarkable are the gilded, baroque altarpiece, and the Renaissance cloisters, decorated with 18th-century *azulejos*.

✚ 37C3
✉ 81km southeast of Porto
ℹ Tourist Office: Avenida Calouste Gulbenkian (☎ 032 422014)

Grão Vasco Museum
☎ 032 26249
🕐 Tue–Sun 9:30–12:30, 2–5. Closed Mon and public holidays
♿ Few
💰 Free on Sun, moderate Tue–Sat

A medieval pillory still stands outside Viseu's imperious Cathedral

Lisbon & Central Portugal

As Portugal's capital city, Lisbon holds a concentration of historical and cultural attractions and is the nation's most cosmopolitan city by far. Standing roughly halfway between north and south, it is also strategically placed for exploring the central regions of Estremadura and Ribatejo.

Estremadura is a region of rocky coast and flat plains, flanked by gentle hills to the north and south, and sprinkled with historic towns such as Sintra and Alcobaça.

The Ribatejo region to the northwest of Lisbon is less culturally rich. However, as it encompasses the flood-plain of the Tagus, its fecundity lies in the alluvial soil, allowing wheat and rice to be grown, and horses and cattle to graze on fertile pastures. The only place of great historical note in Ribatejo is Tomar, where the Order of Christ, successors of the crusading Knights Templar, had their base.

'Porto works and
Braga prays,
Coimbra studies but
Lisbon plays.'

PORTUGUESE
APHORISM

Lisbon

In a country with a reputation for melancholy, Lisbon is proud to call itself the national playground as well as the nation's capital. As a laid-back and attractive city, it makes an excellent short-break destination for tourists.

If you are fit, the steep gradients of the hills over which central Lisbon is scattered are best explored on foot. The most famous part of town is the Alfama district, a labyrinth of cobbled alleys, miniature squares and whitewashed houses, rising in tiers from the Tagus.

The architectural contrast with the nearby, low-lying Baixa district, which was totally destroyed in the devastating earthquake of 1755, is dramatic. This area was rebuilt in precise grid form with magnificent squares and avenues.

Another district which attracts visitors to Lisbon is the Bairro Alto. This is the most bohemian quarter of the city, rising to the west in steep streets and stone staircases, and lined with restaurants, *fado* houses and mildly raffish bars. The lower part of the district, from where several lifts rise to the upper reaches, is the elegant Chiado, with fashionable department stores and tea houses. The area is being painstakingly restored after a serious fire in 1988.

Westwards along the Tagus, the other area of Lisbon not to be missed is Belém. The suburb is home to some of Lisbon's finest Manueline architecture, evoking Portugal's great era of world discovery.

Dom José presides over Lisbon's splendid Praça do Comércio

What to See in Lisbon

CASTELO DE SÃO JORGE ✪✪✪

Crowning a hill surrounded by the Alfama district, the castle is built on 5th-century Visigoth and 9th-century Moorish foundations. The present 12th–14th-century edifice was begun by Afonso Henriques, following his capture of Lisbon from the Moors in 1147. A climb up through the Alfama district to the top is rewarded by stupendous views over the Tagus and its suspension bridge, and by beautiful gardens planted when the castle was restored in 1938.

MOSTEIRO DOS JERÓNIMOS (► 21, TOP TEN)

MUSEU CALOUSTE GULBENKIAN (► 22, TOP TEN)

MUSEU DA MARINHA (MARITIME MUSEUM) ✪✪

This is the place to go if you want to understand how, in the 15th and 16th centuries, Portugal rose to become one of the greatest maritime and trading powers on earth. The museum houses maps, documents, navigational instruments and models of ships from the era of discoveries through to this century. There is also an interesting section on naval aviation.

Did you know ?

The anguished, wailing songs beloved of the Portuguese belong to a musical tradition known as fado. The word means fate, and is unique to Portugal. It expresses the national sense of longing, left behind when the nation's sense of greatness evaporated.

➕ 53D3
🕐 Daily 9–sunset
🚌 Bus 37
♿ Few
🎫 Free

➕ Off map 52A1
✉ Praça do Imperio
☎ 01 362 0019
🕐 Tue–Sun 10–5. Closed Mon and public holidays
🚌 Buses from the Baixa district, tram 15
♿ Few
🎫 Cheap Tue–Sat, free Sun

Above: *the Castelo de São Jorge crowns the Alfama district, and has wide views over the Baixa and beyond*

51

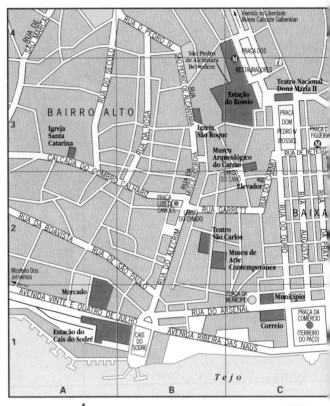

Off map 52A1
Praça Afonso de
Albuquerque, Belém
Tue–Sun 10–5:30. Closed
Mon and public holidays
Buses from the Baixa
district, tram 15
Few
Moderate Tue–Sat, free
Sun

Off map 52A1
Belém
01 301 6228
Tue–Sun 9:30–6:30
Buses from the Baixa
district, tram 15
Good
Moderate

MUSEU DOS COCHES (COACH MUSEUM) ✪✪

Immediately to the east of the Presidential Palace at
Belém, in a former riding school, is this superb collection
of horse-drawn coaches. The collection spans three
centuries and comes from royal households around Europe
including Portugal, Spain, France and Italy.

Some are extremely extravagant and ornate – glittering
with gold and lined with velvet. Pride of place goes to a
sumptuous trio of coaches built in Rome for the
Portuguese ambassador to the Vatican, the better to
project an image of Portugal as a proud and wealthy nation.

PADRÃO DOS DESCOBRIMENTOS ✪
(MONUMENT TO THE DISCOVERIES)

This huge, triumphalist monument was unveiled in 1960 on
the orders of Salazar, to mark the 500th anniversary of
Prince Henry the Navigator's death. Curved to the seaward
side and angular on the other, it also represents the prow of
a ship, and serves as a memorial to all the sailors, patrons
and other players in the Portuguese Age of Discoveries.

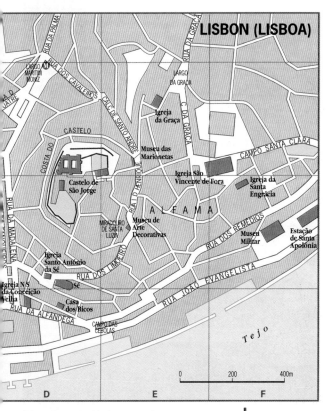

LISBON (LISBOA)

RUA DA PALMA

RUA DA GRAÇA

LARGO MARÍTIMO MONIZ

RUA DOS CAVALEIROS

CALÇ DE SANTO ANDRÉ

LARGO DA GRAÇA

Igreja da Graça

CASTELO

CAMPO SANTA CLARA

COSTA DO

Museu das Marionetas

Castelo de São Jorge

RUA D. HENRIQUE

Igreja São Vincente de Fora

Igreja da Santa Engrácia

A L F A M A

MIRADOURO DE SANTA LUZIA

Museu de Arte Decorativas

RUA DOS REMEDIOS

Museu Militar

Estação de Santa Apolónia

RUA DA MADALENA

RUA DOS LIMOEIRO

Igreja Santo António da Sé

Igreja N/S da Conceição velha

Sé

RUA JOÃO EVANGELISTA

Casa dos Bicos

RUA DA ALFÂNDEGA

CAMPO DAS CEBOLAS

T e j o

0   200   400m

D   E   F

Prince Henry the Navigator stands, appropriately, at the prow. A rapid lift whisks you up to the top, from where there are commanding views over the city: the Tagus estuary spanned by the great 25 de Abril suspension bridge to the west, and the new Vasco da Gama bridge to the east.

At the foot of the monument is a giant mosaic compass and map of the world charting the great voyages of discovery, donated by the government of South Africa in 1960 to demonstrate solidarity with Portugal's colonial policy.

Prince Henry the Navigator gazes across the Tagus from the Monument to the Discoveries

53

Off map 52A1
Calcada da Ajuda
Tours Thu–Tue 10–5.
Closed Wed
Tram 18 from Baixa, or
Bus 14 from Belém
Few

52C1

PALÁCIO DA AJUDA ⚫⚫

Above the pink National Palace of Belém, the official residence of the president of Portugal (not open to the public), is the former Ajuda royal palace, built between 1796 and 1826. It was occupied by the royal family on their return from exile in Brazil, and remained the royal residence until the abolition of the monarchy in 1910.

It is sumptuously furnished with tapestries, sculpture, oriental carpets and historic paintings, and has displays of royal jewellery, crystal and other treasures. The palace is still used for state occasions such as banquets for visiting royalty.

PRACA DO COMÉRCIO ⚫⚫
(Also known by its old name TERREIRO DO PAÇO)

The most splendid of Lisbon's many squares built after the 1755 earthquake is in the centre, giving on to the Tagus, and is lined on three sides with imperious classical façades, most of which are now government buildings.

Left: *Lisbon's Cathedral interior tells the story of Portuguese architecture*
Below: *the Torre de Belém*

SÉ (CATHEDRAL) ✪✪

Like many Portuguese cathedrals, including those at Porto, Évora and the Sé Velha at Coimbra, Lisbon's cathedral was originally a fortress as well as a place of worship. Sturdy twin crenellated towers, rising above the façade, are testimony to this. It was founded in the 12th century following the conquest of the Moors and, from the outside, maintains a distinct Romanesque mien.

The interior tells a fuller story of Portuguese architectural history. The nave is in plain, somewhat austere Romanesque style, but the ambulatory and lancet windows are Gothic. There is a beautiful baroque crib and a fine 17th-century organ.

A side chapel houses the tombs and stone effigies of notables including archbishops of Lisbon and Lopo Fernandes Pacheco, a 14th-century comrade-in-arms of King Afonso IV, with a dog at his feet. Off this chapel are the 13th-century monastic cloisters. A door from the south transept leads into the sacristy, where treasures and religious art are displayed in the Museu do Tesouro da Sé. Try not to miss the mother-of-pearl oriental casket, said to contain relics of St Vincent.

➕ 53D2
✉ Largo da Sé
🕐 Daily 8:30–6. Cloisters Tue–Sun 9–12, 2–6
♿ Few
💲 Church admission free. Cloisters cheap, free on Sun

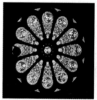

TORRE DE BELÉM ✪✪

This 16th-century fortress on the edge of the Tagus has defended the capital and housed political prisoners; today it is one of Lisbon's most photogenic landmarks, looking almost like a tall ship tethered to the quayside and floating serenely on the river.

Inside is a museum of weapons and armour, and you can climb up to the top of the tower for fine views over the Tagus estuary.

➕ Off map 52A1
✉ Avenida de Brasília
☎ 01 362 0034
🕐 Tue–Sun 10–5
🚋 Tram 15 from Baixa, bus 29, 43 from Belém
♿ None
💲 Oct–May, moderate; Jun–Sep cheap

Lisbon Walk

Distance
3½km

Time
About three hours

Start point
Praça do Comércio
✚ 52C1

End point
Rua Garrett
✚ 52C2

Lunch
Cervejeria da Trindade (££)
✉ 20 Rua da Trindade
(adjacent to Largo do
Carmo)

Start at the Praça do Comércio.

This is Lisbon's bustling centre, also frequently called by its old name Terreiro do Paço, after the royal palace which stood here until its destruction in the 1755 earthquake. It is set on the river with the Castelo São Jorge towering above.

Follow the long, straight, pedestrianised Rua Augusta away from the river. There is frequently an almost carnival atmosphere along here, with street performers and vendors selling flowers, roasted chestnuts and lottery tickets. The road spills into Rossio Square.

Rossio Square is lined with cafés spilling on to the pavement, aflutter with pigeons, and presided over by a statue of the playwright Gil Vincente adorning the façade of the Dona Maria II National Theatre. This is Lisbon at its liveliest; stop a while and watch the world go by.

Rossio Square in Lisbon's Baixa district, an ideal place to sit and watch the world go by

Leave the square via Rua Áurea at the southwest corner. One block along is the iron-girdered Elevador Santa Justa. Take this lift up to the top for glorious views over the city. A bridge leads from the lift, into Rua do Carmo. On the right is the Convento do Carmo.

Wander around the atmospheric ruins of this Carmelite convent which tumbled down in the 1755 earthquake, and was never rebuilt. It is easy to forget that you are in the middle of the city.

Cross to the other side of the Largo do Carmo, turn left into Rua Serpa Pinto, and left again into Rua Garrett.

Named after author Almeida Garrett, this is one of Lisbon's most fashionable and characterful streets. On the left, at number 20, is the famous A Brasileira. This gilt and mirrored coffee house, with a bronze statue of poet Fernando Pessoa outside, simply oozes atmosphere. It has long been a haunt of Lisbon's literary circle.

What to See in Central Portugal

ALCOBAÇA (▶ 16, TOP TEN)

BATALHA (▶ 17, TOP TEN)

CASCAIS ✪✪

Cascais is a smart, large and still-burgeoning holiday resort, surpassed in size on the Lisbon coast only by Estoril. It is also a commuter town for wealthy Lisboetas. Echoing the story of so many fishing ports, especially in the Algarve, the centre of activity is now the tourist trade, with scores of hotels and restaurants, but catches are still unloaded daily on the beach and auctioned in the local market.

58A1
🖂 32km west of Lisbon and 13km from Sintra
ℹ Tourist Office: Rua Visconde da Luz (☎ 01 486 8204)

ESTORIL ✪✪

Portugal's most popular holiday resort north of the Algarve was famous long before the 1960s tourist explosion. Since the end of the 19th century the town has attracted the rich and famous from around Europe, and in the 1940s and 1950s became home to various deposed crowned heads, such as King Humberto of Italy and King Juan of Spain.

Some imposing façades and the casino recall this era, although the other facilities are as up-to-date as anywhere. This combination of an old-fashioned holiday ambience and the new cosmopolitan image, gives Estoril an atmosphere which is the antithesis of quaint. The resort makes annual appearances on the world's television screens, when the Portuguese Grand Prix motor race is held at Estoril's Autodrome, and hosts the Estoril Open ATP tennis tournament.

58A1
🖂 29km from Lisbon
ℹ Tourist Office: Arcadas do Parque (☎ 01 468 0113)

Café society in the smart resort of Cascais, on the Lisbon coast

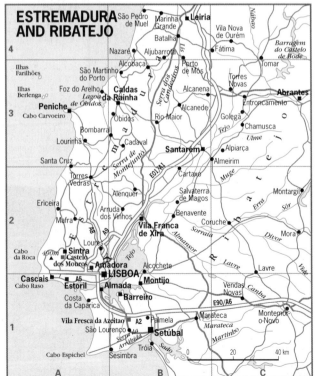

ESTREMADURA AND RIBATEJO

São Pedro de Muel
Marinha Grande
Leiria
Vila Nova de Ourém
Nabão
Barragem do Castelo de Bode

Batalha
Aljubarrota
Fátima

Nazaré
Alcobaça
Porto de Mós
Tomar

Ilhas Farilhões
São Martinho do Porto
Torres Novas
Alcanena

Ilhas Berlenga
Foz do Arelho
Caldas da Rainha
Alcanede
Abrantes

Peniche
Lagoa de Óbidos
Entroncamento

Cabo Carvoeiro
Óbidos
Rio Maior
Golegã
Chamusca

Bombarral
Alpiarça
Ulme

Lourinhã
Cadaval
Santarém

Santa Cruz
Serra de Montejunto
Almeirim

Torres Vedras
Cartaxo
Muge
Montargil

Ericeira
Alenquer
Salvaterra de Magos
Erra
Sôr

Mafra
Arruda dos Vinhos
Benavente
Coruche
Mora
Divor

Loures
Vila Franca de Xira
Sorraia
Almansor

Cabo da Roca
400m
Sintra
Castelo dos Mouros
Tejo
Alcochete
Lavre
Lavre
Vide

Amadora
LISBOA

Cascais
Cabo Raso
A5
Estoril
Almada
Montijo
Vendas Novas
Canha

Costa da Caparica
Barreiro
E90/A6

Vila Fresca da Azeitão
A2
Palmela
Marateca
Montemor-o-Novo

São Lourenço
Serra da Arrábida
Setúbal
Marateca
Martinho

Cabo Espichel
Tróia
Sado

Sesimbra

0   20   40 km

A   B   C

58

Arrábida Coastal Drive

Leave Lisbon via the 2km–long 25 de Abril suspension bridge, leaving the IP1 motorway at the second exit and following the EN378 to Santana. Turn right here, onto the EN379 to Cabo Espichel.

Cabo Espichel is a desolate, wind-fretted cape at the furthest end of a barren plateau. It has a raw beauty to it as you look out over towering, sea-battered cliffs.

Return to Santana, and turn right, twisting down for a couple of kilometres to Sesimbra.

This is the quaintest and most attractive fishing port and resort on the Arrábida coast and consequently has become something of a tourist honeypot. However, sheltered by cliffs and with a sizeable beach, it still has a great deal of charm as well as being excellent for fishing, diving and sailing. There is a castle, originally Moorish, with a small archaeological museum.

Return to Santana and pick up the EN379 again; this time turn eastwards, into the Parque Natural da Arrábida.

This protected nature park covers a string of hills with vineyards, orchards and pine forest, sloping down to some dramatic cliffs in the south.

For the most beautiful scenery, turn right at Aldeia de Irmãos, and wind through the hills on the EN379-1, eventually turning on to the EN10-4, which rejoins the EN379 at Vila Fresca da Azeitão, where you find the wine cellars of Fonseca.

José Maria da Fonseca is one of Portugal's best known wine-makers. The cellars can be visited on a free tour which includes wine-tasting.

Distance/time
75km; 6 hours including stops

Start point
25 de Abril Bridge
✚ 58A1

End point
Vila Fresca da Azeitão
✚ 58B1

Lunch
Nova Fortaleza (££)
✉ Largo dos Bombaldes, Sesimbra

Above: *Sesimbra's fishing fleet lands fresh, deep-water fish and sea food*

Opposite: *ready for picking? A wine-maker inspects the grapes before the wine harvest in the Ribatejo*

59

🔲 58C4
✉️ 20km east of Batalha
ℹ️ Tourist Office: Avenida José Alves Correia da Silva (☎ 049 531139)

🔲 58B4
✉️ 67km south of Coimbra
ℹ️ Tourist Office: Jardim Luís de Camões (☎ 044 823 773)

Castle
🕐 Daily 9–5:30
♿ None
✋ Cheap

🔲 58B3
✉️ 78km northeast of Lisbon
ℹ️ Tourist Office: 63 Rua de Capelo Ivens (☎ 043 391512)
❓ National Gastronomic Fair in Oct/Nov (dates variable)

FÁTIMA ✪✪✪

Fátima is one of the principal places of pilgrimage in the Roman Catholic world. On 13 May 1917 three peasant children saw a vision of the Virgin Mary speaking to them from the top of an oak tree. She warned of cataclysmic events about to take place in Russia, and pleaded for prayer and sacrifice as prerequisites for peace in the world. Further apparitions took place on the 13th day of each subsequent month, culminating in an inexplicable spectacle on 13 October, when 70,000 onlookers saw the sun spinning like a ball in the sky. Many of these witnesses are still alive. Two of the children died soon afterwards but the third, Sister Lucia, still lives as an enclosed Carmelite nun.

The phenomenon sparked a spiritual regeneration in Portugal. Millions visit the site every year, including upwards of 100,000 on 13 May and 13 October. A basilica has been built on the spot of the apparitions with a vast tarmac area where the faithful gather. There are dozens of cheap hotels and hundreds of stalls selling tawdry religious artefacts.

Fátima has nothing for the sceptical. Others find a source of spiritual energy here.

LEIRIA ✪

Leiria is a pleasant little agricultural town on the River Liz, clustering around a perpendicular rock topped by a forbidding medieval castle. Inside a ring of defensive walls, is the sheer keep and the royal palace containing a vast hall. At night, the castle is floodlit and shines out like a beacon for miles around.

ÓBIDOS (▶ 23, TOP TEN)

SANTARÉM ✪

The capital of the Ribatejo region is a bustling town on the west bank of the Tagus, which serves as the agricultural hub for the fertile outlying plains. These days Santarém is best known for being the bullfighting and dressage capital of Portugal. Fine specimens of both bulls and horses are to be seen grazing in the rich pastures surrounding the town – horsemanship was developed as a means of fighting the bulls by mounted *cavaleiros*.

However, Santarém is not a place to linger, unless you happen to be there during the last week in October or first week in November (it differs from year to year), when the great National Gastronomic Fair is held, and you can wander from stall to stall tasting regional titbits from all over Portugal, amid fireworks and jollity.

TORRES VEDRAS ⭐

The famous 'lines of Torres Vedras' feature prominently in Peninsular War textbooks. They consist of three rings, each of about 100 fortified hilltops, built in 1809–10 by the Anglo-Portuguese forces under Wellington, to defend Lisbon from Napoleon's armies. Some of the walls, ditches and gun emplacements are still intact and can be identified from the N8 road; a scramble up also guarantees a view over the bumpy hills to the next fortification in the line on either side.

The best place to see the remains of the lines is from a reconstructed fort which stands just outside the town of Torres Vedras. There is unrestricted access to the lines, 24 hours a day, all through the year.

✚ 58A2
✉ 34km south of Óbidos

The Lines
♿ None
✋ Free

Flamboyant flourishes, typical of Manueline architecture, reflect Portugal's great maritime exploits

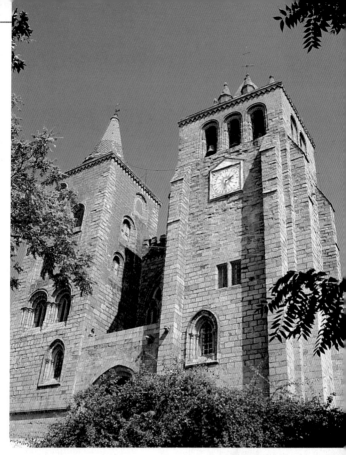

SÉ (CATHEDRAL) ✪✪✪

Cross to the opposite side of the square, beyond the Roman temple, to appreciate the full glory of the 12th- and 13th-century façade, and the two huge, dissimilar towers built 400 years later. On the way in, do not miss the carved stone statues of the 12 apostles guarding the entrance. In the soaring nave, vast chandeliers hang from the vaulted ceiling.

A staircase at the back leads to the cathedral's Museum of Sacred Art, which houses a glittering collection of treasures including crucifixes and offertory chalices in gold and silver, the vestments and mitres of full episcopal pomp and ceremony and – by far the most beautiful exhibit in the museum – a 13th-century carved ivory statue of the Virgin of Paradise.

The 14th-century Gothic cloisters are reached through a door in the cathedral nave. Climb any of the corner staircases up onto the battlements for wonderful views over the town, and the plains of the Alentejo beyond.

✚ 69C2
✉ Largo Marquês de Marialva
☎ 066 26910
🕐 Church always open; museum Tue–Sun 9–12, 2–4:30. Closed Mon and public holidays
♿ Few
💲 Church free; museum cheap

Above: *Évora's Cathedral, one of the wonders which make the city a World Heritage Site*

71

Évora Walk

Distance
2km

Time
3–4 hours

Start point
Largo Marquês de Marialva
🔲 69B2

End point
Praça do Giraldo
🔲 69B2

Lunch
O Focardo (££)
✉ Rua dos Mercadoes 6

Start outside the Convento dos Lóios (➤ 68) on the Largo Marquês de Marialva square, at the centre of which is a Roman temple.

The remains of this temple, built in the second century AD, constitute the most outstanding Roman monument in Portugal. Parts of it have been dismantled for other building works over the centuries, but six of the Corinthian-style columns on marble plinths are perfectly intact. It is particularly beautiful floodlit at night.

Before leaving the square, also check out the cathedral and municipal museum (➤ 69, 71). Walk under an arch behind the cathedral apse, and turn left to follow down a narrow street to the Antiga Universidade (Old University).

Walk around the cool, two-storey cloister and admire the fine *azulejo* tiles in the lecture rooms.

Walk down narrow Rua Conde da Serra da Tourega, turning left into Largo das Portas de Moura, where there is a fine, Manueline stone fountain, shaped as a globe. Notice the splendidly ornate façade of Casa Cordovil. Walk back across the square to Igreja da Misericórdia.

Above: Now under protection, Évora's unique Temple of Diana was previously used as a market place

Misericórdia is worth seeing for the fine baroque altar, and *azulejo*-embellished walls.

Return to Largo das Portas de Moura, this time turning right on to Rua Miguel Bombarda and left onto Rua da República, down to Igreja São Francisco (➤ 70). Walk back up Rua da República, and left up the hill into Praça Do Giraldo.

Opposite: the Convento da nossa Senhora de Conceiçao in Beja, scene of a passionate love affair

Évora's main square, Praça do Giraldo, is cobbled with black and white *paralelo* stones, and arcaded round the sides, leaving open-air cafés coolly shaded.

What to See in the Alentejo

BEJA ✪✪

Reputedly the hottest place in Portugal, but a pleasant town with several points of historical interest. The 15th-century **Convento da Nossa Senhora de Conceição** (on Largo Nossa Senhora de Conceiçao) is one of the most beautiful buildings in the Alentejo. It was here that the convent's most famous resident, Sister Mariana Alcoforado, had a love affair with a French count in the 17th century. Her piously erotic letters were later published as *Letters of a Portuguese Nun*.

74B2
60km south of Évora
Tourist Office: 25 Rua do Capitão J F de Sousa (☎ 084 23693)

Convento
Tue–Sun 9:45–12:30, 2–5:15. Closed Mon
Cheap

ESTREMOZ ✪✪

Ancient, fortified Estremoz, rising out of the Alentejo flatness, has a medieval atmosphere, felt particularly by those who stay in the 13th-century royal castle which dominates the town, and which has been turned into a most extraordinary *pousada*.

But just as important a part of Estremoz's fascination is to be discovered as you wander along the historic streets, many of them cobbled, between Moorish squares and past imposing façades. Rising above the royal palace section of the castle is the white marble Torre das Três Coroas (Tower of the Three Crowns), so-called because kings Sancho II, Afonso III and Dinis all contributed to its construction. The climb up a steep, worn staircase to the top of the keep is rewarded by a 360-degree panorama as far as Évora, and across to Spain in the east, if the weather is clear.

Within the keep is the beautiful **Capela Rainha Santa Isabel**, adorned with *azulejo* tile paintings recounting the life of this 14th-century queen and saint who dedicated her life to the poor, often in defiance of her husband King Dinis. She died in the town in 1336.

The castle is always open; a key to the chapel is available in the summer.

74C3
44km northeast of Évora
Tourist Office: 26 Largo da República (☎ 068 333541)

Castle keep and chapel
None Moderate

Eastern Alentejo Drive

A scenically spectacular alternative to the busy main roads between Évora and the Algarve is to take the remote, back roads near the Spanish border.

Turn off the main IP2 at Beja, taking the 260 eastwards to Serpa.

Serpa is a fine place to stop and feel the soul of the Alentejo. The old quarter is dwarfed by the rambling ruins of a fortress and old city walls. But the real joy of the town is to wander the ancient streets lined with whitewashed houses, which more than anywhere evoke the spirit of the Moors.

Take the 260 road eastwards out of town. After just 2½km, pull over at the pousada *on the right, and ask at reception for the key to the Capela São Gens.*

This simple chapel, with its plain columns inside, is believed to be one of only two original Moorish mosques surviving intact in Portugal. It is worth enjoying the hushed atmosphere of its cool interior for a few moments. Then, if it is lunchtime, try the *pousada* for good Alentejo cuisine.

Continue on the 260, then bear right on to the 265, crossing the open plains towards the ridge of mountains to the east. The country becomes increasingly wild and remote-feeling, as the road becomes twistier, and you approach Mértola.

Spectacularly perched on a narrow gorge, Mértola is at the River Guadiana's highest navigable point. Curiously, in the village is Portugal's other mosque – now the Igreja Matriz.

Meander on down the Guadiana valley on the 122 road, until you cross into the Algarve shortly past the village of Espírito Santo, and head for the resorts of the south coast.

Distance
260km

Time
5–8 hours, depending on stops

Start point
Évora
🚩 28B2

End point
Faro, Algarve
🚩 28B1

Lunch
Restaurante Alengarve (£)
✉ Avenida Aureliano Fernandes, Mértola
☎ 086 62210

Above: *Mertola's cobbled streets are deserted during hot, summer siesta-time*

Left: *cork oaks in the Alentejo*

75

Food & Drink

A traditional Portuguese meal is a big, lusty affair involving several courses.

There are many regional variations and specialities. However, there is one food in particular which unites the national palate – *bacalhau*, or dried, salted cod. There are many different ways of preparing it, such as *Gomes de Sá* (in layers with diced potatoes, onions, olives and hard-boiled egg); and *conde de guarda* (creamed with mash and cabbage).

Many Portuguese meals begin with a bowl of steaming soup. One to look out for is *caldo verde* – cabbage shredded finely and flavoured with garlic sausage.

Fish and seafood are also much favoured and abundantly available, particularly in coastal towns. *Camarões* (shrimps), *gambas* (prawns), *sapateiro* (giant, hairy crab) and *lagosta* (lobster), all caught in the cold, deep Atlantic, are wonderful and very pricey. Among the best fresh fish are *espada* (scabbard fish), *carapau* (horse mackerel), *linguado* (sole), and of course the ubiquitous *sardinhas* (sardines). *Pescada* (hake) can be good, too, but make sure it is *fresca* (fresh) not *congelada* (frozen).

Sardines can be sizzling on the charcoal barbecue within minutes of landing on Portimão's quayside

The meat dishes in Portugal may be presented as a casserole or grilled on a skewer, be it *bife* (steak), *porco* (pork), *frango* (chicken) or *cabrito* (kid). In the north, stew is often cooked and served in an earthenware pot called a *pucara*. *Frango na pucara*, for example, is a chicken casserole. In the south, particularly the Alentejo, the hinged, metal *cataplana*, which snaps shut like a clam and sizzles with anything the cook has decided to put in, is widely seen. Sometimes, meat and fish appear in the same dish, for example in dishes such as *cataplana alentejana*, which has both shellfish and pork in it. This is a particularly delicious combination.

Wines and Port

Port is Portugal's most famous liquid export. In Vila Nova de Gaia, opposite Porto, it is available for tasting free of charge in the many shippers' houses (► 26).

In general, Portuguese table wines emulate the food in being good, honest, characterful and unencumbered by

A tortuous road now leads up to the craggy summit, where a *pousada* has been built among the handful of tightly clustered houses within the walls, which can be walked round for stupendous views over to Spain.

MONSARAZ (► 20, TOP TEN)

VILA VIÇOSA ✪✪

This royal city was once the seat of the Dukes of Braganza, the family which provided Portugal with its monarchs from 1640 until the proclamation of the Republic in 1910. It is worth stopping at, to visit the **Paço Ducal (Ducal Palace)**, whose 110m-long marble façade forms one side of the main square.

The palace is now a museum, filled with huge paintings depicting Portugal's military triumphs – particularly those over the Spanish – along with displays of fine art, porcelain, tapestries and other treasures from the royal era. Also worth seeing are a collection of royal carriages and the kitchens, where enormous, gleaming copper cauldrons and huge roasting spits evoke the era of royal hunting and feasting.

➕ 74C3
✉ 18km southeast of Estremoz
ℹ Tourist Office: Praça da República (☎ 068 881101)

Paço Ducal
☎ 068 98659
🕐 Tue–Sun 9–1, 2–6. Closed Mon and public holidays
💷 Expensive

Vila Viçosa, once a favourite haunt of royalty

The Algarve

When Portuguese from elsewhere in the country say *Algarve não é Portugal* – 'The Algarve is not Portugal' – they are referring to several factors which separate this province from the rest of the country. The main difference is the strong Moorish influence to the culture; architecture, food, place-names, words in local dialects and even the physical appearance of some Algarvians.

The other main difference is the Mediterranean-type climate which the Algarve enjoys. This, of course, is what has been responsible for the explosion in tourism, turning an agricultural and fishing-based economy into one dependent on holiday-makers from northern Europe, in a single generation.

'...the Algarve... is not Andalusia's far west, but Portugal's deep south. It should be visited first by the foreigner who has already been in Portugal for several months.'

HENRY MYHILL,
British traveller
(1969)

Faro

Faro is the capital of the Algarve, whose airport, just west of the city, is the main gateway for the several million tourists who visit the south coast resorts every year. It is built at the edge of a wide lagoon surrounded by wetlands and salt flats, 10km from a vast beach splintered into sandy islands, some of which emerge and disappear with the tide.

Faro Cathedral, whose side chapels are adorned with 17th- and 18th-century tiles

Faro was an important Moorish city which was captured by Afonso III in the dying days of Arab rule in Portugal. It continued to flourish until 1596 when, under Spanish occupation, the town was sacked and burnt by the British. In 1755 it was again destroyed – this time by the great earthquake, more famous for having reduced Lisbon to rubble. But despite this, an attractive walled old town and a few historic monuments survive, warranting an incursion into the heart of the city.

What to See in Faro

CAPELA DOS OSSOS (CHAPEL OF BONES) ✪✪
Like its better-known counterpart in Évora, the walls of this small, ghoulish ossuary in the crypt of the Igreja do Carmo are lined with human bones and the grinning skulls of long-deceased monks, reminding visitors of the certainty of their death.

🕇 89D1
✉ Largo do Carmo
🕐 Mon–Sat 10–1, 3–5
♿ None
🍴 Moderate

MUSEU MARÍTIMO (MARITIME MUSEUM) ✪
This museum, housed in the harbour master's office on the seafront, is dedicated to the industry on which Faro's prosperity has depended for centuries – fishing. Models of numerous vessels demonstrate the evolution of the fishing boats and have been recreated with infinite care and detail. Rooms full of other fishing equipment are also on display, including crab and cuttlefish traps and harpoons for spearing shark and tuna.

🕇 89D1
✉ Rua Comunidade Lusiada
☎ 089 803601
🕐 Sun–Fri 2–5. Closed Sat and bank holidays
♿ Few
🍴 Cheap

SÉ (CATHEDRAL) ✪✪
A jumbled mixture of Gothic, Renaissance and baroque of no great architectural distinction. However, the 17th- and 18th-century *azulejos* in the side chapels on both sides of the nave are worth seeing. The darkened interior can also be deliciously cool on a hot day.

🕇 89D1
✉ Largo da Sé
🕐 Mon–Fri 10–12. Sat and Sun, open only during services
ℹ Tourist Office: Rua da Misericórdia (☎ 089 80360)
♿ Few
🍴 Free

> ### Did you know ?
> Faro was sacked and burnt by the Earl of Essex in 1596. Although England and Portugal were allies at the time, this was the period of annexation by Spain, with whom Britain was at war.

Above: *chapel in the grounds of Igreja do Carmo, better known for its Chapel of Bones*

Faro Walk

Distance
3km

Time
2–4 hours, depending on stops

Start point
Jardim Manuel Bivar
✚ 89D1

End point
Museu Marítimo
✚ 89D1

Lunch
Restaurante O Gargalo (£££)
✉ 30 Largo do Péda Cruz
☎ 089 27305

Storks alight on the highest points they can find, such as the belfry of Faro's Igreja do Carmo

Start at Jardim Manuel Bivar

These well-tended gardens look out across the harbour and are the only part of town where there is some sense of peace and open space as seabirds call and halyards clink on masts.

From the south end of the gardens, enter the old town through the stone arch next to the Turismo. This is the 18th-century Arco da Vila, with its statue of Thomas Aquinas. A short walk along the Rua do Município leads into the Largo da Sé (Cathedral Square) and the Sé itself (➤ 83).

Cross the Praça Afonso and leave the old town through the Arco de Repousa, turning left into Rua Manuel Francisco, then right at the crossroads into Rua Santo António main shopping street and left at the Praça da Liberdade, onto Rua de Portugal. Adjacent to the end of this road is a white-fronted building housing the Teatro Lethes.

Inside the former Jesuit college of Santiago Maior, now the Teatro Lethes, is a chapel converted into a tiny replica of La Scala, Milan's famous opera house. The building stages varied art and other exhibitions.

Cross the Largo das Mouras Velhas and turn right up Rua do Sol, then left, crossing Rua do Alportel into Largo do Poço, which leads into Largo do Carmo.

In the middle of Largo do Carmo stands the Igreja do Carmo, a Carmelite church, whose alluring, if macabre, feature is the Capela dos Ossos (➤ 83).

Return to the Largo do Poço, and follow the Rua Alistão Vardim as far as Rua 1 de Maio. Turn right here, rejoining the harbour at Praça Francisco Gomes, at the north end of Jardim Manuel Bivar. Walk round the north of the harbour, ending at the Museu Marítimo (➤ 83).

What to See in the Algarve

ALBUFEIRA

Albufeira has become a symbol of the transformation, within a single generation, of the Algarve's fishing communities into a string of metropolises catering for huge numbers of sun-seeking tourists from northern Europe.

However, Albufeira still retains much of its original quaint charm. There are cobbled streets and whitewashed cottages squatting at the feet of apartment blocks; hidden away, there are two simple, rather lovely, old churches – Capela de Misericórdia (Chapel of Mercy) and the Igreja de São Sebastião (Church of Saint Sebastian); down on the beach there are still fishermen who draw their gaily-painted wooden boats up onto the sand and sell their catches by Dutch auction.

CABO DE SÃO VICENTE (► 18–19, TOP TEN)

LAGOS

History-packed Lagos is among the most attractive of the Algarve's coastal towns. To a large extent it has survived the advent of tourism with its charm intact, because most of the development has been outside the town.

In Praça Infante Dom Henrique there is a large bronze statue of Henry the Navigator holding his sextant and gazing out to sea. Leading off from the square are cobbled, pedestrianised streets lined with cafés, bars and restaurants where you can sit and eat or drink *al fresco* while enjoying the cheerful ambience.

📏 88C2
✉ 39km west of Faro
ℹ Tourist Office: Rua 5 de Outubro (☎ 089 512144)

Above: *Albufeira is the ultimate fishing village turned mega-resort*

📏 88B2
✉ 16km west of Portimão
ℹ Tourist Office: Largo Marquês de Pombal (☎ 082 763031)

88B3

Monchique is 25km north of Portimão

MONCHIQUE ✪✪

The best day to visit the main town of the Monchique hills is the third Friday of every month, when there is a large market with farmers from a wide area bringing their produce for sale, as well as ceramics and handicrafts. At other times, visitors find a quiet, elegant little town, once they have penetrated the encircling, tacky modern outskirts.

The highest peak in the Algarve is 902m Foia, 8km from Monchique and topped by ugly broadcasting masts. There is nothing else up here apart from souvenir stalls, but on a clear day the views are sensational, as are the sunsets.

88B2

62km west of Faro

Tourist Office: Largo 1 de Dezembro, Portimão (☎ 082 23695) and Avenida Tomás Cabreira, Praia de Rocha (☎ 082 22290)

PORTIMÃO ✪

Portimão is surrounded by an ugly urban sprawl, though there are a few points of interest for those who penetrate the centre, such as the Largo Primero de Dezembro, and the fine Igreja Matriz. There is also excellent shopping on the cobbled walkways between Rua do Comércio and Rua Vasco da Gama.

Down by the port next to the old bridge across the Arade, is a string of waterside cafés and simple restaurants where you can eat charcoal-grilled sardines and other fish, as fresh as any you are ever likely to try.

Portimão's beach is at Praia da Rocha (2km from town), which, in the early days of the Algarve's tourism, was the jewel of the coast, magnificently overhung by red sandstone cliffs and pitted with numerous caves. The huge beach of fine sand is strewn with rugged outcrops sculpted by nature into weird formations and backed now by huge hotel complexes.

Opposite: *nature has sculpted extraordinary forms on Praia da Rocha*

Below: *fresh sardines with salad and bread are irresistible to holidaymaking diners*

SAGRES ✪✪✪

The small town where Prince Henry the Navigator set up his famous School of Navigation is right out on the very corner of Europe. The scenery is suitably dramatic: solid, bare, windswept bluffs with steps hewn out of them lead down to beaches where the tide washes round in great sweeps, while gulls swirl and hover high above.

✚ 88A1
✉ 33km west of Lagos
ℹ Tourist Office:
Promontório de Sagres
(☎ 082 64125)

Western Algarve Drive

Distance
165km

Time
4–6 hours including stops

Start point
Lagos
✠ 88B2

End point
Lagos
✠ 88B2

Lunch
Praia do Castelejo
beach café (£)

*Start from Lagos. Take the 125 westwards,
signposted Sagres (▶ 87). Continue 6km along
the cliff-top road, to Cabo de São Vicente
(▶ 18–19). Return to the road junction just
above Sagres, and take the 268 northwards,
signposted to Vila do Bispo. Go through this
village, and take the unmade road immediately
north, signposted to Praia do Castelejo.*

The huge beach of Praia do Castelejo is backed by high
cliffs and gets few visitors. The sea is rough and often
cold, tempting only a few dedicated surfers. However, it is
an excellent place to appreciate the raw beauty of the
western Algarve, and to lunch in the beach café.

*Return to Vila do Bispo, and continue north on
the 268 to Aljezur.*

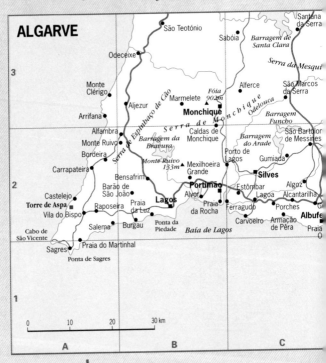

Elsewhere in Europe, the old town of Aljezur, topped by a ruined castle, might have a turnstile, official guide and ice-cream stall. But climb to the castle for wonderful views over the west coast, and you will probably have the place to yourself.

From Aljezur, take the 267 inland (eastwards), into the gentle green Monchique hills, to the town of Monchique (➤ 86). Four kilometres south of Monchique, just off the 268, is the pretty spa town of Caldas de Monchique.

Caldas de Monchique is where the ubiquitous Monchique mineral water comes from. On the main square are some fine old façades belonging to the era of 19th-century gentility when the spa was popular with wealthy Spaniards. Some delightful trails lead off into the woods, from just behind the square.

The 268 continues south, through orchards and citrus groves, rejoining the 125 west of Portimão. Turn right to return to Lagos.

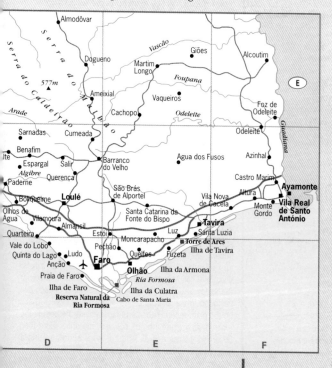

SILVES ★★★

Silves was the old Moorish capital of the Algarve, recaptured by Christian forces in 1249. It was an Atlantic port until the River Arade, on which it stands, silted up. The aura of the Moors lives on, as you will discover if you take a walk round the old, restored castle walls. Also worth seeing is the 13th-century Sé de Santa Maria (Cathedral), and the **Museum of Archaeology**, which puts the town's history into context.

88C2
✉ 7km northeast of Portimão
ℹ Tourist Office: Rua 25 de Abril (☎ 082 442255)

Museum of Archaeology
✉ Rua das Portas de Loulé
☎ 082 444832
🕐 Mon–Sat 10–12:30, 2–5
💰 Moderate

TAVIRA (► 25, TOP TEN)

VALE DO LOBO ★★

A modern, up-market, purpose-built tourist complex of over 750 luxury villas, swimming pools, restaurants, boutiques, nightclubs, tennis courts (including the famous David Lloyd Tennis Centre), next to some of the Algarve's finest golf courses. It is all very beautifully done in typical low, domed, whitewashed Algarvian architectural style. The resort has everything except local culture and a beach; for these, residents have to leave the complex gates and brave the real world.

89D1
✉ 15km west of Faro

VILAMOURA ★★

The most extensive tourist complex in Portugal. Vilamoura started off as a development of posh villas around a superb golf course; now there are four 18-hole courses and a wide range of villas, apartments and hotels. Vilamoura has neither the exclusive air of Vale de Lobo nor the seediness of Albufeira, although elements of each can be found in the sharply contrasting 'villages' which make up the giant resort. The sports facilities are the best in the Algarve; as well as the golf courses, there are more than 50 tennis courts and all kinds of watersports around a huge marina with over 1,000 berths.

89D2
✉ 26km west of Faro

Above: tourists peruse the local lace in Silves, the ancient Moorish capital of the Algarve

Where To...

S VICENTE

The North

Prices

Approximate prices for a three-course meal for one person are shown by £ symbol:

£ = budget, under Esc1500

££ = moderate, Esc1500–3,000

£££ = expensive, over Esc3,000

Amarante

Zé da Calçada (£££)

Some think this restaurant overpriced for good though not outstanding food. On the other hand the view over the stone bridge and town are superlative and a treat to savour.

✉ Rua 31 de Janeiro
☎ 055 422023

Barcelos

Casa dos Arcos (££)

Good homely cooking with excellent bread and fish. Don't even think of coming without making a reservation if it is a Thursday (that is, market day).

✉ Rua Duques de Bragança
☎ 053 811975 🔘 Closed Mon

Braga

A Toca (£)

Highly recommended for a lunchtime snack if you are sightseeing in the town. Sandwiches, savoury and sweet pastries, plus a *prato do dia* (dish of the day) are all served here.

✉ 127 Rua do Souto
☎ 053 23279

Bragança

Lá em Casa (££)

Best place in town to eat. *Lá em casa* means 'at home'. Bearing this in mind, the fish and meat dishes are surprisingly elaborate.

✉ Rua Marques de Pombal
☎ 073 22111

Coimbra

Cozinha (££)

Cosy, exceptionally friendly and family-run. Homely Portuguese cooking including top-notch *bacalhau Gomes de Sá* (sliced and served with potatoes and hard boiled eggs).

✉ Rua Azeiteiras 65
🔘 Closed Mon

Trovador (££)

Rather formal restaurant, with a country-house atmosphere and tiled walls. Good traditional food at fair prices.

✉ Largo da Sé Velha 17
☎ 039 25475

Zé Manel (££)

The atmosphre is jaunty and studenty during the academic term, and the restaurant remains popular, though more sedately so, during vacation time. The *cabrito* (kid) is excellent.

✉ 12 Beco do Forno
☎ 039 23790

Guimarães

O Telheiro (££)

Good standard food with fast service, so a particularly good bet if you are trying to get round the sights in a hurry. As an alternative, there is a good café, Dom João, located on the floor below.

✉ 39 Rua Dom João I

Porto

Avó Miquinhas (££)

Ride the tram along the waterfront to Castelo do Queijo, then take a short taxi ride to this excellent, reasonably-priced fish and seafood restaurant by the marina in Leça.

✉ Rua do Castelo 81, Leca da Palmeira ☎ 02 995 3330
🔘 Closed Mon

Café Majestic (£)

A wonderful 18th-century gilt and mirrored city centre café. Perfect for a snack lunch.

✉ Rua da Santa Catarina 112
☎ 02 2003887

Filha da Mãe Preta (££)

Richly atmospheric and mildly raunchy restaurant on the quayside. If you are brave enought to risk trying *tripas à Portuguesa* (tripe with beans), this is the best place to do it.

✉ Cais da Ribeira 39

O Escondidinho (£££)

To most gourmet tastes, this is the very best Porto has to offer in the way of traditional fare. Perhaps inevitably, it has the reputation of being a bit cliquey.

✉ Rua Passos Manuel 114
☎ 02 2001079   Closed Sun

Portucale (£££)

Superb views can be enjoyed from the penthouse plus top-notch international cuisine and modern interpretations of traditional dishes.

✉ 598 Rua da Alegria
☎ 02 570717

Restaurante Chinês (£££)

Superb Cantonese food is served in this authentic restaurant run by immigrants from Portugal's colony of Macau. Just on the Porto side of the Dom Luis I bridge's upper level, there are great views across to Vila Nova de Gaia.

✉ Avenida Vimara Peres 38
☎ 02 200 8915

Taverna dos Bebóbos (££)

Traditional Porto and Minho fare down on the quayside.

A long established restaurant, but now very popular with tourists.

✉ Cais da Ribeira 24
☎ 02 313565

Valença do Minho

Pousada de São Teotónio (£££)

For your first or last meal in Portugal coming from, or *en route* to, Spain, have it here with views across the Minho. Excellent regional cuisine.

☎ 051 824020

Viana do Castelo

Tres Arcos (£££)

The place to come if you want to sample superb, fresh Atlantic seafood – and pay through the nose for it, of course.

✉ Largo JT da Costa 25
☎ 058 24014
  Closed Mon

Tres Potes (££)

A large, lively restaurant serving lusty Minho fare, as well as fish and seafood. Attracts many tourists on Fridays and Saturday nights, when there are sometimes folk dance shows. It's essential to book ahead at weekends and during the high season.

✉ Beco dos Fornos 7
☎ 058 829928

Vila Real

Espadeiro (££)

Vila Real's top restaurant, which serves excellent *bacalhau*, trout and suckling pig. There is also an extensive wine list.

✉ Avenida Almeida Lucena
☎ 059 322302

Tripas

Porto's most famous regional dish, *tripas à Portuguesa* (tripe with beans) is not for the squeamish. It could be said that this plateful of white, leathery internal organ is to *nouvelle cuisine* what Vasco da Gama was to ballet dancing.

Lisbon & Central Portugal

Bread

The universal staple in Portugal is the crusty roll known as a *pãozinho* in the north, and a *papo seco* in Lisbon and the south. The coarse and heavy but characterful *broa* is made from maize, rye or corn meal.

Alcobaça

Trindade (££)

Right by the abbey and an excellent place to round off a sightseeing session.

✉ **22 Praça Dom Henriques**
☎ **062 42397** ◉ **Closed Sat**

Batalha

Pousada do Mestre Afonso Domingues (£££)

The *pousada*, right next to the monastery, serves a fine meal, preceded by delicious cured ham and cheesy titbits.

☎ **044 96260**

Cascais

Cascais (£)

Good value, no frills family restaurant serving hearty portions of plain food.

✉ **4 Beco dos Invalidos**
☎ **01 483 3734**

João Padeiro (£££)

Some of the best seafood on the Lisbon coast served in convivial surroundings.

✉ **Rua Visconde de Luz 12**
☎ **01 483 0232** ◉ **Closed Mon**

Estoril

Pak Yun (££)

Hugely popular Chinese restaurant and deservedly so. Booking ahead is advisable.

✉ **Rua de Lisboa 5**
☎ **01 467 0691**

Leiria

Restaurante Jardim (££)

Good regional food, which includes grilled trout, served in view of both the river and the castle.

✉ **Jardim Luis de Camões**

Lisbon

Aviz (£££)

Goes from strength to strength with high quality Portuguese and international food.

✉ **Rua Serpa Pinto 12B**
☎ **01 342 8391** ◉ **Closed Sat lunch and Sun**

Bota Alta (£)

A small, simple restaurant at the heart of the Bairro Alto serving good, hearty food.

✉ **Travessa da Queimada 34–7**
☎ **01 3427959**

Cantinho do Aviz (£)

A Mozambican restaurant in the Alfama district, serving unusual African food.

✉ **Rua Lourenço Marques 3**
☎ **01 876472** ◉ **Closed Sun**

Carvoeiro (£)

Serves freshly grilled fish with homemade bread and wine by the jug.

✉ **Rua Vieira Portuense 66–68**
☎ **01 3637998**

Casa de Pasto Alentejana (£)

A tile-decorated café near Rossio square serving simple meals and snacks.

✉ **2 Praceta Goa**
☎ **01 9219717**

Gambrinus (£££)

Best place in the Baixa district for seafood and fresh fish.

✉ **Rua Portas de Santo Antão 25** ☎ **01 34 21466**

Garghalada (££)

Good value international cuisine in a friendly atmosphere with good service. Just beneath Castelo São Jorge.

✉ **Rua do Castelo 7**

Forno Velho (££)

A first rate Brazilian restaurant serving large plates of barbecued meats and *feijoada* (bean stew).

✉ **Rua do Salitre 42, Avenida da Liberdade**

O Caseiro (£££)

Top place in Belém to eat good, unpretentious food. Very near Jerónimos monastery.

✉ **35 Rua de Belém** ☎ **01 363 8803**

Sua Exelencia (££)

Romantic little restaurant in the Lapa district, where the owner frequently introduces himself personally to guests.

✉ **40–2 Rua do Conde** ☎ **01 60 3614** ◎ **Closed Wed**

Tágide (£££)

One of Lisbon's top restaurants, located on fashionable Rua Garrett. High class international cuisine.

✉ **Largo da Académia National de Belas Artes 18** ☎ **01 34 20720** ◎ **Closed Sun**

Varinha da Madragoa (££)

Large portions of good, traditional Portuguese dishes, including Alentejo specialities. Good value for money.

✉ **Rua das Madres 36** ☎ **01 396 5533** ◎ **Closed Mon**

Óbidos

Muralhas (££)

Fashionable and arty visitors to Óbidos come here for high quality, traditional Portuguese cooking.

✉ **Rua Dom João de Ornelas** ☎ **062 959836**

Pousada do Castelo (£££)

A richly atmospheric and romantic place in which to dine. It's also very popular and can get busy, so reserving a table is highly recommended.

☎ **062 959105** ◎ **Closed Tues**

Peniche

A Gaivota (££)

Enjoy a lunch made with fresh fish which has been landed just hours earlier, as you gaze across the water towards the Berlenga Islands.

✉ **Avenida do Mar** ☎ **062 782202** ◎ **Closed Mon**

Santarém

O Mal Cozinhado (£)

Excellent value food served in this restaurant, which has a lot to live up to, as it is located in the town which holds an well-regarded annual gastronomic fair.

✉ **Campo da Feira** ☎ **043 23584**

Sintra

Cantinho de São Pedro (£££)

Top quality French and Portuguese cuisine served at a restaurant with high standards, and prices to match.

✉ **18 Praça Dom Fernando II** ☎ **01 923 0267** ◎ **Closed Mon and Wed evening**

Tacho Real (££)

This restaurant serves a selection of excellent food, both Portuguese and international, at reasonable prices.

✉ **Rua da Ferreira 4** ☎ **01 923 5277** ◎ **Closed Mon**

Nibbles

Saucers of locally cured meats, cheese, almonds, olives and other titbits frequently arrive, unsolicited, on restaurant tables. These are not generally 'free' – you pay as you pick, with prices shown on the menu. Sometimes, however, particularly in *pousadas*, they are included in the *table d'hôte* prices. To clarify matters, point to them and ask if they are '*incluido?*'

Alentejo

Pork and Clams

Porco à Alentejana, a speciality of the region, is one of Portugal's most interesting dishes, consisting of pork stewed with clams. One theory is that the dish originated in the 15th-century when Jews were expelled from Portugal or forced to convert to Christianity. They were served this dish to test whether they had really severed links with the old faith.

Beja

Alentejano (££)
Real, as opposed to designer-tourist Alentejo food is served here. Locals favour the brimming bowls of soup and big hunks of pork.
📧 6–7 Largo dos Duques de Beja ☎ 084 23849

Casa Primavera (£)
The pick of Beja's many inexpensive restaurants, Casa Primavera is family-run and very friendly.
📧 19 Largo do Correio
☎ 084 25980

Pensão Tomas (££)
Excellent *porco à Alentejana* (pork with clams) among other southern specialities.
📧 7–11 Rua Alexandre Herculano ☎ 084 324613

Elvas

Canal 7 (£)
The best of a large number of cheap restaurants, conveniently located where much international road traffic stops to eat.
📧 Rua dos Sapateiros 16
☎ 068 623593

Centro Artistica Elvense (£)
An excellent place to come for a quick, tasty snack or the more substantial dish of the day. Located next to the bus station.
📧 Praça da Republica

O Aqueduto (££)
Excellent fish – which is an unusual boast for a Portuguese restaurant set so far inland.
📧 Avenida da Piedade
☎ 068 623676

Estremoz

Aguias d'Ouro (££)
Wholesome, homely local fare at reasonable prices.
📧 Praça Rossio 27 ☎ 068 333326

Pousada da Rainha Santa Isabel (£££)
High class Alentejan food with superb views from the dining room at one of Portugal's finest *pousadas*.
☎ 068 332075

Évora

A Muralha (£)
Good café serving excellent *pasteis de carne* (meat pastries) and other snacks.
📧 Rua 5 de Outubro 21
☎ 066 22284

Cozinha de Santo Humberto (£££)
The finest food you'll find in Évora. Very attentive service and excellent wine list. It's certainly expensive, but well worth it.
📧 Rua da Moeda 39

Luar de Janeiro (££)
A small, cosy restaurant with a formal touch.
📧 Travessa de Janeiro 13
☎ 066 24895

Martinho (££)
Trendy restaurant with arty flourishes, serving original interpretations of traditional Alentejo dishes.
📧 24–5 Largo Luis de Camoes
☎ 066 23057

O Antão (££)
Modern restaurant which also exhibits the work of local artists.
📧 Rua João de Deus 5–7
☎ 066 26459

WHERE TO EAT & DRINK

Pousada dos Lóios (££)

An unforgettable experience: eating in the cloisters of this fabulous, converted 15th-century monastery.

✉ **Largo Conde de Vila Flor**
☎ **066 24051**

Restaurante Típico Guiao (££)

Very popular restaurant whose *ementa Turistica* is good value.

✉ **Rua da República 81**
☎ **066 23071**

Marvão

Pensão Dom Dinis (££)

A small and friendly establishment. Good and cheaper alternative to dining at the *pousada*.

✉ **Rua Dr Matos Magalães**
☎ **045 93236**

Pousada de Santa Maria (£££)

This is by far the best place to eat in Marvão, if only for the quite stupendous panorama out over the Alentejo plains.

✉ **7 Rua 24 de Janeiro**
☎ **045 93201**

Monsaraz

Horta da Moura (£££)

One of the joys of summer in the Alentejo is eating outside on the patio of this hotel, below the impressive town walls.

✉ **Reguengos de Monsaraz**
☎ **066 550100**

Solar de Monsaraz (££)

You are sure of a warm welcome in this friendly, family-run eatery. The food is unsophisticated, but very filling.

✉ **38 Rua Conde de Monsaraz**

Serpa

Alentejano (££)

Specialities at this restaurant include rich, meaty dishes and several excellent local ewe's milk cheeses, all at reasonable prices.

✉ **Praça da República**
☎ **084 53335**

Cuiça-Filho (£)

Cheap, cheerful and exceptionally friendly, family-run restaurant.

✉ **Rua Portas de Beja 18**
☎ **084 90566**

Vila Nova de Milfontes

Miramar (££)

This is probably the best of the resort's many inexpensive restaurants. Good fish.

✉ **Largo Brito Pais**

Portal da Vila (£££)

If money is no object, come to the Portal da Vila, order a big, fresh lobster and a couple of bottles of chilled white wine, and have done with it.

✉ **Rua Sarmento Beiras 5a**

Vila Viçosa

Framar (£)

Simple restaurant run by a friendly family. Large portions at very reasonable prices.

✉ **35 Praça da República**
☎ **068 98158**

Ouro Branco (££)

A good selection of Alentejo dishes is on offer at this restaurant, including excellent soup.

✉ **Campo da Restauração**

Local Wines

The Alentejo is gradually emerging as a leading wine-growing area, for both reds and whites. Esporão, Redondo and Borba are all names to look out for.

Algarve

Menus

In certain tourist areas, the law requires restaurants to offer a three-course *menu turistica*, inclusive of drinks and coffee, at a set price. While these can be good value (particularly if you see locals tucking into them), too many places seem to have settled on a monotonous routine of vegetable soup, grilled hake (frozen) and ice cream.

Albufeira

A Ruína (££)
Good fresh fish and seafood dishes, served on the beach side.
✉ **Cais Herculano**
☎ **089 512094**

Atrium (£££)
The place to splash out for a posh, romantic meal with a good variety of fish, international cuisine and an excellent wine list.
✉ **Rua 5 de Outubro** ☎ **089 515755**

Cabaz da Praia (££)
Enjoy some fine views over the sea from the restaurant's terrace, while choosing from the large, mainly fish-based menu.
✉ **Praça Miguel Bombarda**
☎ **089 512137**

Tasca Viegas (££)
This is the closest thing you are likely to find in Albufeira to a typically Portuguese restaurant.
✉ **Cais Herculano 2**
☎ **089 514087**

Faro

A Tasca (£)
An excellent, very traditional tavern, of a kind which is usually hard to find in the Algarve.
✉ **Rua do Alportel 38**
☎ **089 824739**

Cidade Velha (££)
A pleasant and cosy restaurant, which is well located, in Faro old town. The menu offers a selection of traditional southern cuisine.
✉ **Rua Domingo Guieiro 19**
☎ **089 27145**

Dois Irmãos (£££)
This is generally considered to be one of Faro's best restaurants, serving a range of excellent fish and seafood dishes.
✉ **Largo Terreiro do Bispo 20**
☎ **089 27145**

Tasco O Chalaver (££)
A cheerful, character-rich taverna frequented by locals, many of whom are there just to drink. It has a big barbecue, where fresh fish and meat are grilled on charcoal.
✉ **Rua Infante D Henrique**
☎ **089 822455**

Lagos

Alpendre (£££)
Delicious sole and other fish. Booking essential in summer.
✉ **Rua António Barbosa Viana 17** ☎ **082 762705**

Dom Sebastião (£££)
A very popular, top-notch restaurant, serving a wide range of international and southern Portuguese dishes. Be sure to book ahead, especially in summer.
✉ **20–2 Rua 25 de Abril** ☎ **082 762795**

Piri-Piri (££)
Unsurprisingly, the speciality here is hot, spicy chicken *piri-piri*. It goes well with cold beer.
✉ **Rua Alfonso d'Almeida 10**

O Celeiro (££)
Excellent restaurant, worth the journey out of town. Delicious nibbles served with pre-dinner drinks.
✉ **On the left of the N125 between Lagos and Sagres**
☎ **082 69144** ◎ **Closed Mon**

O Lamberto (££)
Rise above the fray on a street lined with restaurants spilling onto the pavement, and eat comfortably on a first floor terrace.

🖂 **Rua 25 de Abril**
☎ **082 763746**

Monchique

A Charrette (££)
The pick of several rather touristy restaurants catering for the day-tipper trade. Serves some good rice dishes.

🖂 **Rua Samora G**

Portimão

A Lanterna (££)
Comprehensive range of Algarvian and Alentejo specialities. Good atmosphere and service.

🖂 **On the east side of the old bridge** ☎ **082 414429**

Iemanjá (££)
Rather bizarre-looking little restaurant, themed as a cave. Good fish.

🖂 **Rua Serpa Pinto 9**
☎ **082 23233**

O Bicho (££)
Very popular with locals and probably the best place in town for genuine Portuguese food.

🖂 **Largo Gil Eanes 12**
☎ **082 22977**

Praia de Luz

A Concha (££)
An attractive restaurant, where you can dine in comfort under a shady pergola. The food is well prepared here, if somewhat predictable.

🖂 **6 Avenida dos Pescadores**

Sagres

A Tasca (££)
Fresh fish and enchanting views of the harbour.

🖂 **At the port** ☎ **082 64177**

Pousada do Infante (£££)
You need time for a long, leisurely lunch or dinner here. Excellent food and cliff top location.

☎ **082 64222**

Silves

Mesquita (££)
A cosy, friendly little restaurant serving reliable local food.

🖂 **Rua Policarpo Dias**
☎ **082 442747**

Rui I (£££)
A traditional, very busy *masisqueira* serving seafood under bright lighting.

🖂 **Rua Comendador Vilarinho 27** ☎ **082 442682**
🕐 **Closed Tue**

Tavira

Imperial (££)
Well known for its big, fresh, meaty fish steaks.

🖂 **Rua José Pires Padinha 22**
☎ **081 22306** 🕐 **Closed Wed**

O Caneção (£££)
A delightful, if pricey, quayside restaurant, where you can watch the fishing fleet sail in and feast on fresh fish and seafood.

🖂 **162 Rua José Pires Padinha**
☎ **081 819211**

Petisqueira Belmar (££)
Small, family-run restaurant serving a good value *prato do dia* (dish of the day).

🖂 **16 Rua Almirante Cándido dos Reis** ☎ **081 324995**

Snacks
Cafés are an excellent bet for cheap snack lunches. Nationwide standard fare includes *rissois de camarão* (shrimp rissoles), *bolinhos de bacalhau* (deep fried cod balls), *pregos* (steak sandwiches) and a panoply of sweet and gooey wonders.

The North

Prices
Approximate prices per room per night, regardless of double or single occupancy

£ = budget, under Esc8,000

££ = moderate Esc8,000–15,000

£££ = expensive, over Esc15,000

Alijó

Pousada de Barão Forrester (£££)
Superb *pousada*, recently given a face lift. Surrounded by port vineyards.
✉ **Rua José Rufino**
☎ **059 959215**

Amarante

Hotel Navarras (££)
A good and comfortable three-star hotel, convenient for all the town's major sights.
✉ **Rua Murtas-Madelena**
☎ **055 422106**

Barcelos

Quinta do Convento da Franqueira (££)
A beautiful Turismo de Habitacão in a sea of Vinho Verde vineyards, next to a ruined monastery about 5km from Barcelos. The English owners rent just three rooms. Booking ahead is essential.
✉ **Pereira** ☎ **053 831606**

Braga

Hotel Sopete Parque (££)
A fine old four-star hotel, which has recently been renovated. Friendly and comfortable.
✉ **Parque de Bom Jesus do Monte** ☎ **053 676548**

Bragança

Hotel Bragança (££)
A friendly, good value three-star hotel, conveniently located in the centre of town and providing excellent service.
✉ **Avenida Francisco Sá Carneiro** ☎ **073 22578**

Pousada de São Bartolomeu (£££)
Modern *pousada*, which has the added advantage of wonderful views over the castle.
✉ **Estrada do Turismo**
☎ **073 331493**

Buçaco

Palace Hotel do Buçaco (£££)
Luxury hotels do not come much more bizarre than this royal extravaganza, which is incongruously set in a dense forest.
✉ **Buçaco** ☎ **031 930101**

Coimbra

Bragança (££)
A wonderfully located hotel, which is absolutely packed with good, old-fashioned charm.
✉ **Largo das Ameias 10**
☎ **039 22171**

Quinta das Lágrimas (£££)
Travellers who want to get away from the hustle and bustle can enjoy a relaxed stay in this peaceful, characterful old house.
✉ **Santa Clara** ☎ **039 441615**

Guimarães

Pousada de Santa Marinha da Costa (£££)
A richly atmospheric *pousada* in a converted monastery.
☎ **053 514453**

Mangualde

Casa d'Azurara (£££)
Delightful old country house, with 15 luxuriously furnished rooms.
✉ **Rua Nova 78** ☎ **032 612010**

Pinhão

Casa de Casal dos Loivos (£££)
This is a stupendously positioned, antique-stuffed Turismo do Habitacão house with swimming pool, set among vineyards and overlooking a broad sweep of the Douro Valley. Extremely popular, so an advance reservation is essential.
✉ Casal dos Loivos ☎ 054 72149

Ponte de Lima

Albergaria Império do Minho (££)
A convenient and pleasant base for exploring the Minho on the river. Has a good restaurant, and a swimming pool.
✉ Avenida 5 do Outubro ☎ 058 741158

Casa de Sabadão (££)
A beautiful old house. Excellent base for exploring the Minho.
✉ Arcozelo ☎ 058 941963

Porto

Albergaria Miradouro (££)
A comfortable, friendly place to stay. In the same building as the penthouse Portugale restaurant, one of Porto's best.
✉ Rua da Alegria 598 ☎ 02 570 717

Boa Vista (££)
Surprisingly, this is Porto's *only* hotel with a sea view. Small and charming, though out of the way at Foz do Douro.
✉ Esplanada do Castelo 58 ☎ 02 6183175

Hotel São João (££)
A comfortable three-star, conveniently located for the centre of town, and for the Ribeira district.
✉ Rua do Bom Jardim 120 ☎ 02 200 1662

Infante de Sagres (£££)
Porto's only grand, sumptuous, old-style hotel. Antique-stuffed rooms and immaculate service.
✉ Praça Dona Filipa de Lencastre 62 ☎ 02 2008101

Malaposta (£)
Convenient location, comfortable rooms and good value.
✉ Rua da Conceição 80 ☎ 02 2006278

Pensão dos Aliados (£)
City centre, good service and reasonable prices.
✉ Rua Elisio de Melo 27 ☎ 02 2004853

Viana do Castelo

Casa dos Costa Barros (££)
Family-run inn with just 10 rooms. Very friendly and personal.
✉ Rua de São Pedro 22–28 ☎ 058 24383

Pousada do Monte de Santa Luzia (£££)
Famous old hotel, now a *pousada*. Amazing views over the Minho coast.
✉ Monte de Santa Luzia ☎ 058 828889

Viseu

Grão Vasco (££)
Old-fashioned hotel, revelling in the heritage of artist Grão Vasco.
✉ Rua Gaspar Barreiros ☎ 032 423511

Turismo de Habitacão
This is a nationwide scheme designed to accommodate tourists in private houses in rural Portugal. Typically this will be an old country house with just two or three guest rooms, usually with private bathrooms. Breakfast is included but whether dinner is provided is up to the hosts. Often if guests want an evening meal they simply join the family table.

Lisbon & Central Portugal

York House
York House in Lisbon is so called because in the last century it belonged to two ladies from Yorkshire in northern England. Despite this, it is as Portuguese as can be, bedecked with *azulejo* tiles and full of Portuguese antique furniture.

Alcobaça

Hotel Santa Maria (£)
This modest, friendly and reasonably priced hotel is the best of a very limited choice of lodgings in town.
✉ **Rua Dr Franciso Zagalo**
☎ **062 597 395**

Cascais

Hotel Albatroz (£££)
A superb, if very pricey, smallish luxury hotel in a converted palace. The old rooms have more character, but a new wing offers greater comfort.
✉ **Rua Federico Arouca** ☎ **01 284 4827**

Palma (£)
A charming, very friendly, little *pensão*. Good value for money.
✉ **Avenida Valbom 15**
☎ **01 4837797**

Estoril

Hotel Atlantico (££)
A fine, four-star seaside hotel; the south-facing rooms have excellent sea views.
✉ **Estrada da Marginal**
☎ **01 468 3619**

São Cristovão (££)
Beautiful, very small seafront *pensão* which has managed to retain its character.
✉ **Avenida Marginal**
☎ **01 4680913**

Fátima

Dom Gonçalo (£)
A charming little inn, full of pilgrims.
✉ **Rua Jacinta Marto 100**
☎ **049 533062**

Hotel de Fátima (££)
Although a touch lacking in character, this four-star hotel is the largest and most comfortable place to stay in Fátima.
✉ **Rua João Paulo II** ☎ **049 532 351**

Lisbon

Alegria (£)
Very friendly, fairly basic *pensão* conveniently located in the Baixa.
✉ **Praça da Alegria 12**
☎ **01 3475522**

Avenida Palace (£££)
Classical, old-style opulence and superlative service.
✉ **Rua 1 Dezembro 123**
☎ **01 3460151**

Hotel da Lapa (££)
A sybaritic hotel, each room individually styled, in the quiet Lapa district.
✉ **Rua do Pau da Bandeira 4**
☎ **01 3950005**

Hotel Lisboa Plaza (££)
A very good standard four-star, conveniently and centrally located.
✉ **Travessa do Salitre 7** ☎ **01 346 3922**

Hotel Palácio do Estoril (£££)
The old-fashioned, though stylish, five-star hotel, where the crowned heads of Europe have hob-nobbed over the decades.
✉ **Rua do Park** ☎ **01 468 0400**

International (££)
Very comfortable and reasonably priced, though not particularly strong on character.
✉ **Rua da Betesga 3**
☎ **01 3466401**

Lar do Arreiro (£)
Comfortable and excellent
value. Near the bullring.
⊠ Praça Dr Sá Carneiro 4
☎ 01 8493150

**Residencial Principe Real
(££)**
Small, friendly and good
value. The restaurant serves
traditional Lisbon dishes.
⊠ Rua da Alegria 53
☎ 01 3460116

Roma (£)
Pleasant little *pensão*, near
the Avenida da Liberdade.
⊠ Travessa da Gloria 22a
☎ 01 3477621

Suiço Atlântico (£)
Quiet, comfortable old-style
hotel at the heart of the
Bairro Alto.
⊠ Rua da Glória 3–19
☎ 01 3469013

Tivoli Lisboa (£££)
A famous hotel, offering
elegance and sophistication.
⊠ Avenida da Liberdade 185
☎ 01 353 0181

York House (£££)
Converted monastery
offering the atmosphere of a
country *quinta*.
⊠ Rua das Janelas Verdes 32
☎ 01 3962435

Óbidos

**Albergaria Rainha Santa
Isabel (££)**
A modest place with a
friendly atmosphere and
rooms with balconies
overlooking a narrow street.
⊠ Rua Direita ☎ 062 959 247

**Estalagem do Convento
(£££)**
A former convent
immediately outside the main
gate into the walled town,
which is the most
atmospheric place to stay if
you can't get into the
pousada.
⊠ Rua João de Ornelas
☎ 062 959217

Pousada do Castelo (£££)
Portugal's smallest *pousada*,
and one of the most romantic
places in the country to stay.
☎ 062 959105

Palmela

Pousada de Palmela (£££)
Glorious *pousada* within
ancient stone walls. Superb
views over the Arrábida
peninsula.
⊠ Castelo de Palmela 2950
☎ 01 2351226

Queluz

**Pousada da Dona Maria I
(£££)**
A wonderful *pousada*, and
very convenient for visiting
the Peninsular War battle
sites.
⊠ Largo Palácio de Queluz
☎ 01 4356158

Sintra

Palácio de Seteais (£££)
A converted 18th-century
palace of overwhelming
grandeur, set in spectacular
gardens.
⊠ Rua B du Bocage 8
☎ 01 9233200

Tomar

Estalagem Santa Iria (££)
Enchanting little inn on an
island. Convenient for the
town sites and for river
walks.
⊠ Parque do Mouchão
☎ 049 321238

Pousadas
Pousadas are state-run
inns and hotels, which
make up an excellent
network of
accommodation outside
the cities. Several are
national monuments;
others are modern, but
built at historic sites. A
third category are modern
lodges built in locations
chosen for their wild
remoteness and wonderful
views.

103

Alentejo

Lusitanos

Several fine, thoroughbred *Lusitano* horses are stabled at the Horta de Moura hotel in Monsaraz. They can be ridden across the Alentejo plain from here. *Lusitanos* were originally bred for bullfighting, and are today most famous for dressage.

Beja

Pousada de São Francisco (£££)
Splendidly converted, 13th-century monastery.
✉ **Largo Dom N Alvares Pereira** ☎ **084 328441**

Residencial Cristina (££)
Modern, friendly, good value hotel, conveniently located.
✉ **Rua de Mertola 71**
☎ **084 323035**

Elvas

Pousada de Santa Luzia (£££)
A comfortable, modern *pousada* outside the walls. There is a good restaurant serving, as in all *pousadas*, traditional local specialities.
✉ **Avenida de Badajoz**
☎ **068 622194**

Quinta de Santo António (£££)
Exquisite old inn, luxuriously restored.
✉ **São Bras** ☎ **068 628406**

Estremoz

Pousada da Rainha Santa Isabel (£££)
A touch austere perhaps, but this is the closest most people in the modern world get to the atmosphere of a medieval castle.
✉ **Largo Dom Dinis**
☎ **068 332075**

Évora

Pensão Policarpo (££)
An atmospheric, if somewhat faded hotel, with friendly service and good value.
✉ **16 Rua da Freira de Baixo**
☎ **066 22424**

Pousada dos Lóios (£££)
Another atmospheric *pousada*. Sleep in the monastic cells and dine in the cloisters.
✉ **Largo do Conde de Vila Flor** ☎ **066 24051**

Solar Monfalim (££)
A fine old town centre house, with comfortable rooms and a convenient location.
✉ **Largo da Misericordia 1**
☎ **066 22031**

Marvão

Pousada de Santa Maria (£££)
Quite simply one of the most sensationally located *pousadas* in Portugal: hence the high prices.
✉ **Rua 24 de Janeiro**
☎ **045 93201**

Monsaraz

Estalagem de Monsaraz (£)
Simple but friendly and peaceful inn below the city walls.
✉ **Largo de São Bartolomeu**
☎ **066 55112**

Horta de Moura (£££)
Relaxing and very comfortable hotel designed in farmhouse style and set on the plain below Monsaraz.
✉ **Reguengos de Monsaraz**
☎ **066 550100**

Redondo

Convento de São Paulo (£££)
A cool, history-packed oasis out on the sunbaked plains of the Alentejo.
✉ **Aldeia da Serra**
☎ **066 999100**

Algarve

Albufeira

Residential Vila Branca (£)
Small and comfortable. The best of Albufeira's budget hotels.
✉ **Rua do Tenis 4** ☎ **089 586804**

Faro

Casa de Lumena (£)
Faded but rather charming old town house set around a courtyard.
✉ **Praça Alexandre Herculano 27** ☎ **089 801990**

Hotel Eva (£££)
Faro's top hotel with spacious rooms overlooking the harbour and sea.
✉ **Avenida da Republica** ☎ **089 803354**

Lagos

Pensão Mar Azul (££)
Small, very friendly, good value *pensão* in the middle of town. It can be quite noisy, but is especially recommended during the off-season months.
✉ **13 Rua 25 de Abril** ☎ **082 769143**

Pensão Rubi-Mar (£)
Good, friendly little budget hotel. About the best value in Lagos.
✉ **70 Rua da Barroca** ☎ **082 763165**

Loulé

Loulé Jardim (£)
A small, peaceful hotel. A particularly good place to feel the traditional spirit of the Algarve.
✉ **Praça Manuel de Arriaga** ☎ **089 413094**

Monchique

Residencial Miradouro da Serra (£)
A small, modest place, but the best that Monchique has to offer. Very friendly management.
✉ **Rua dos Combatentes do Ultramar** ☎ **082 921163**

Portimão

Penina (£££)
A very famous golf hotel: this is where the Beatles stayed during the 1960s. It now belongs the Meridien group.
✉ **PO Box 146 – between Portimão and Lagos** ☎ **082 415415**

Praia da Rocha

Pensão Pinguim (££)
A little inn which has been here since before the tourist explosion and has kept its charm.
✉ **Avenida António Feu** ☎ **082 24308**

Sagres

Pousada do Infante (£££)
With its quite sensational location on the bluffs of Sagres, this *pousada* is set in one of the wildest spots of the Algarve.
✉ **Ponta de Sagres** ☎ **082 64222**

Tavira

Convento de Santo António (££)
Beautiful converted monastery, with views extending across the marshes.
✉ **Atalaia 56** ☎ **081 325632**

Azulejos
Glazed, hand-painted tiles, or *azulejos*, are found all over Portugal, particularly in the south. This art form – usually, though not always in blue – is a direct legacy of the Moors. *Azulejos* decorate churches, railway stations and ordinary homes. The best *azulejo* souvenirs are square-shaped paintings on panels of 16 or 25 tiles.

Shopping in Portugal

Pottery

Traditional Portuguese pottery starts at a base level with the ubiquitous cockerels of Barcelos and bawdy creations found in rural markets. Better value is the *barro* glazed earthenware crockery available all over the country. At the top end of the market is the internationally famous *Vista Alegre* porcelain, still much cheaper in Portugal than in the many countries to which it is exported.

Handicrafts and Souvenirs

Albufeira

Infante Dom Henrique House
An extensive range of pottery and other handicrafts.
✉ **Rua Candido do Reis 30**
☎ **089 593267**

Faro

Main Street
There are three branches of this shop, all on the same street. Between them, they offer just about any local handicraft, gift or souvenir you could want.
✉ **Rua Santo António 10, 21 and 29**

Lisbon

Casa das Cortiças
Every different kind of cork product imaginable is on sale here.
✉ **4 Rua da Escola Politécnica**

Casa Quintão
Includes an impressive selection of Arraiolas and other rugs.
✉ **Rua Ivens 30**

Casa Regional da Ilha Verde
A comprehensive range of handicrafts, including a number of items from Madeira.
✉ **Rua Paiva de Andrade 4**

Centro de Turismo e Artesanato
A wide range of ceramics, glass, leather and other handicrafts, from all over Portugal. Packing and shipment can be arranged.
✉ **Rua Castillo 61B**

Madeira Superbia
A fine selection of embroidered clothing, tablecloths and tapestries, all from Madeira.
✉ **Avenida Duque de Loulé 75A**

Pavilhão de Madeira
Another shop selling embroidery and other handicrafts fashioned in Madeira.
✉ **Avenida de Liberdade 15**

Loulé

Bicas Velhas
Excellent for simple pottery. Watch the potters at work at their wheels.
✉ **Rua das Bicas Velhas**

Caldeiraria Louletana
All kinds of copper goods. Huge choice of kitchenware includes *cataplanas*.
✉ **Rua da Barbaça**

Monchique

Casa dos Arcos
Monchique's speciality is simple, folding wooden chairs. They are easily transportable and this is the place to buy some of the best.
✉ **Estrada Velha**

Portimão

Arraiolas
Arraiolas rugs from the Algarve, and many other examples of woven handicrafts.
✉ **Rua Teofilo Braga**

Bazar-Miriamis
A great range of handicrafts and ceramics of all kinds, from the Algarve and elsewhere in Portugal. Shipment of goods can be arranged.
✉ **Largo do Dique 11**

Porto
Ribeira Craft Centre
Very touristy but a comprehensive selection of artefacts from rugs to ceramics, mainly from the Minho and elsewhere in the north.
✉ **Rua da Reboleira 37**

Clothes

Lisbon
Ana Salazar
Several attractive selections from Lisbon's top fashion designers.
✉ **Rua do Carmo**

Custódia
Excellent selection of interesting and original knitwear, designed by Senhora Custódia.
✉ **Rua Rodrigo da Fonseca 113**

Jewellery

Évora
Miranda Ferrão
Local gold and silver work including examples of filigree work.
✉ **Rua 5 Outubro 28–9**

Lagos
Mogador
Good value gold and silver filigree work.
✉ **Rua Gil Eanes**

Terracotta
This is an excellent place to visit for items such as marcasite rings, bracelets and necklaces, as well as other jewellery.
✉ **Praça Luis de Camões**

Lisbon
Casa Batalha
A long established jewellers' shop which offers a surprisingly modern selection of jewellery, as well as their more traditional repertoire of goods.
✉ **Rua Augusta 222 and Amoreiras shopping centre**

Ourivesaria Aliança
A varied and substantial selection of beautiful Portuguese gold and silver filigree work.
✉ **50 Rua Garrett**

W A Sarmento
This is one of Lisbon's longest established goldsmiths, offering a beautiful selection of jewellery. The firm can also prepare work to individual commission.
✉ **Rua do Ouro 251**

Porto
Josephus
Beautiful displays of high quality gold and silver filigree, both traditional and modern. Also a good selection of semi-precious stones. Conveniently and centrally located near the Bolhão covered market.
✉ **Rua Formosa 344**

Pedro A Batista
Silver specialists with a good range of free-standing ornaments, as well as good quality jewellery. Located near the central São Bento station.
✉ **Rua das Flores 235**

Tavira
Stárte
This rather small jewellers' outlet offers a good quality and unusual selection in the more inexpensive sector of the market.
✉ **Rua Guilherme Gomes Fernandes 26**

Baskets
Portuguese woven baskets are worth bringing home. In the north they are known as *seiras* and are made from rushes dyed bright colours. Algarvian baskets are often woven from palm fronds.

Bawdy Pots

The widespread availability of pornographic pottery may shock the more prudish. However, it does allows you to glimpse the earthy side of Portuguese humour. Don't believe any earnest nonsense about 'fertility symbols'. The truth is, it's just plain bawdy!

Glass, Porcelain and High Quality Ceramics

Porches

Casa Algarve

One of the best of many local ceramics shops along this stretch of road, with an endless array of artefacts.

✉ **On the north side of the EN125**

Olaria Pequena

One of Porches's smaller ceramics shops but offering an exquisite selection of goods.

✉ **On the north side of the EN125**

Porches Pottery

The Algarve's most famous ceramics centre, which features many *avante-garde* creations, as well as traditional Algarvian pottery. There is also a selection of cork work.

✉ **On the south side of the EN125**

Portimão

O Aquario

A very smart shop selling a selection of Atlantis crystal glass, Vista Alegre porcelain and other quality products.

✉ **Rua Vasco da Gama**

Porto

Vista Alegre

The famous porcelain manufacturer's main outlet in the city.

✉ **Rua Candido dos Reis**

Lisbon

Atlantis

A full range of Atlantis crystal.

✉ **Amoreiras Shopping Centre, Avenida Duarte Pacheco**

Fábrica Ceramica Viúva Lamego

Hand-painted tiles straight from this factory which also has a shop. Some good deals on seconds.

✉ **Largo do Intendente**

Fábrica de Loiça de Sacavem

Tile paintings and other hand-painted ceramics.

✉ **Avenida da Liberdade 49–57**

Vista Alegre

Vast selection of the famous Vista Alegre tableware.

✉ **Largo do Chiado, 18**

Vista Alegre

More of the same.

✉ **Amoreiras Shopping Centre, Avenida Duarte Pacheco**

Sant'Anna

High quality ceramics and hand-painted tiles.

✉ **91 Rua do Alecrim**

Antiques

Lagos

Casa da Papagaio

Large, rambling selection of bric-à-brac which is sure to delight the dedicated browser.

✉ **Rua 25 Abril**

Lisbon

Fundacão Ricardo do Espirito Santo

Massive selection of high-class reproduction furniture, silverware, tiles and Arraiolas rugs. Shipment can be arranged.

✉ **Largo das Portas do Sol, 2**

Solar

A lot of high-class merchandise, including antique tiles.

✉ **68–70 Rua Dom Pedro V**

Xairel
Paintings and assorted artefacts.
⊠ Rua D Pedro V

Portimão
A Tralha
Assorted antiques, plus a selection of Madeira embroideries.
⊠ **Rua Vasco da Gama**

Casa da Papagaio
Smaller version of sister-shop in Lagos.
⊠ **Rua Santa Isabel**

Porto
Reis Filhos
Very smart, expensive city-centre shop selling antique furniture, leather and modern tableware.
⊠ **Rua da Santa Catarina**

Wine

Faro
Pousada Porto
Best wine shop in Faro, including an excellent selection of Alentejo wines.
⊠ **Rua do Bocage 50**

Lisbon
Solar do Vinho do Porto
The place to buy port in the capital.
⊠ **45 Rua São Pedro de Alcântara**

Portimão
Casco Garrafeira
Good selection of vintage wines and port from all over Portugal.
⊠ **Rua João de Deus 24**

Tio José
Includes an interesting variety of local liqueurs, such as *medronho* distilled from arbutus.
⊠ **Praça da República**

Porto
Solar do Vinho do Porto
If you haven't stocked up on port over the bridge in the lodges of Vila Nova de Gaia, here's another chance.
⊠ **Quinta da Maceirinha, Rua de Entre Quintas 220**

Markets

Barcelos
One of the largest and most famous markets in Portugal.
◎ **Thu**

Espinho
A large market selling handicrafts, ceramics, clothes and food.
⊠ **19 km south of Porto**
◎ **Mon**

Lisbon
Flea Market
The capital's largest outdoor market for handicrafts, clothes, food, rugs and much more. Behind São Vincente church.
⊠ **Campo de Santa Clara**
◎ **Tue, Sat**

Monchique
Farmers from a wide area bring their produce here, as well as ceramics and handicrafts aimed principally at tourists from the coastal resorts.
⊠ **Third Fri of every month**

Ponte de Lima
A colourful market in the Minho.
⊠ **Second Mon of every month**

Porto
Bolhão Market
Colourful, covered market selling food and handicrafts.
⊠ **Corner of Rua Formosa and Rua da Sá de Bandeira**
◎ **Mon–Fri**

Medronho
A bottle of *medronho*, available in wine shops, is guaranteed to bring memories of Portugal flooding. This colourless, burning firewater is distilled from arbutus, a little berry rather like a wild strawberry.

Children's Attractions

Break the Ice
To travel with youngsters can be an excellent way to break the ice with locals. Children are the object of a great deal of attention in Portugal, and are constantly admired and asked after.

Many visitors to Portugal, particularly those from northern European countries, are surprised by the way children are treated and catered for here.

On a superficial level, children's facilities are fairly minimal. There are few theme parks, zoos or other traditional forms of juvenile entertainment. There are, however, plenty of fun fairs to be found throughout the summer months: the Feira Popular in Lisbon; the Feira do Porto at the Palacio Cristal and countless motley collections of ageing dodgems, ferris wheels and candy-floss stalls at *festas* all over the country.

The big difference in Portugal, however, is the way children are indulged – some would say over-indulged. Elderly and young, men and women all make a tremendous fuss over children and make allowances for their needs in hotels, restaurants, shops or museums. While visiting a restaurant for dinner, for example, it is not uncommon for a baby to be whisked off to the kitchen to the delight of chef and staff, while parents carry on with their meal in peace.

Entertaining children in Portugal tends to be a less formal and more pragmatic business – a question of attitude, rather than of provision of specific facilities.

The great majority of children's entertainment in Portugal is located in the Algarve region.

Mini–Golf Courses

Portugal is a top golfing venue, and provides a few mini-golf courses to give aspiring young players a little practice, before they attempt the country's major courses.

Albufeira
Mini-Golfe das Acoteias
✉ Turistico Aldeias de Acoteias

Portimão
Mini-Golfe Hotel Algarve
✉ Praia da Rocha
☎ 082 415001

Vilamoura
Mini-Golfe Dom Pedro
✉ Hotel Dom Pedro
☎ 089 389802

Ten Pin Bowling

There are many ten-pin bowling alleys along the coast, several of them with lighter balls suitable for youngsters.

Albufeira
Aldeamento Turístico Areias de São João
✉ Areias de S João
☎ 089 589231

Apartado Turístico Vale Navio
✉ Sitio do Vale Navio
☎ 089 589254/5

Clube Praia da Ouro
✉ Praia da Oura
☎ 089 589135

Hotel Alfamar
✉ Praia da Falésia
☎ 089 501351

Vila Galé
✉ Galé ☎ 089 591224

Lagos
Hotel Golfinho
☎ 082 769900

Portimão
Hotel Dom João II
✉ Alvor ☎ 082 459157

Vilamoura
Hotel Dom Pedro Golf
☎ 089 389650

Capital Fun

Lisbon
Feira Popular de Lisboa
Fun fair open every afternoon and evening throughout the summer months.
✉ Avenida da República
☎ 01 7934593

Jardim Zoológico
Not the most exciting of zoos, but the best Portugal can offer.
✉ Estrada de Benfica 158
☎ 01 7269349

Theme Parks

Coimbra
Portugal dos Pequenitos
Although this university town is on the whole a rather dry and stuffy place for children, this theme park featuring models of Portugal's best known sights and monuments can provide a little light relief.

Water Parks

In recent years, aquatic parks have enjoyed an explosion in popularity along the Algarve coast. A multitude of them has now been developed, lining the EN125 main highway, most of them located between Faro and Portimão.

Albufeira
Zoomarine
This aqua park features various different marine shows, including the ever-popular performing dolphins.
✉ EN 125 Guia
☎ 089 561104

Lagoa
Slide and Splash
A huge complex of water chutes, slides and swimming pools to keep the water-babies amused.
✉ EN125, Vale Judeu, Estombar ☎ 082 341685

Montegordo
Pinguim
A smaller variation on the water park theme and probably not worth a special journey.
✉ Next to the campsite at Montegordo ☎ 081 511837

Quarteira
Aqua Show
More watery fun of the same order.
✉ EN 396, off the main road

Atlântico Park
Another complex of rides and entertainments that come with a guarantee that participants will get absolutely soaking wet.
✉ EN 125, Quatro Estradas – at the crossroads with the road into Quarteira ☎ 089 397757

Silves
The Big One
Another huge water park, The Big One is fully equipped with a variety of rides, tunnels and wave machines.
✉ EN125, Alcantarilha
☎ 082 322827

Eating Out
In Portugal, children of any age are welcome pretty much anywhere their parents are, including cafés and restaurants at any time of the day or night. Portuguese children tend to sleep during the afternoon and stay up very late.

Discos, Nightclubs & Casinos

African Rhythms
Portugal's home-grown rock music has made few international in-roads. However, it is significantly influenced by African music, brought to Lisbon by musicians from the former colonies of Angola, Mozambique, Guinea-Bissau, São Tome and Principe, and the Cape Verde Islands. Bands include GNR and Sétima Legião.

Discos and Nightclubs

Albufeira

Kiss
Wild and popular club, which is always packed to the gunnels from midnight to 4AM in summer.
✉ **Motechoro**

Kream
A busy, throbbing disco which usually plays techno music.
✉ **Rua do Prior 38**
🕐 **Open till 4AM**

Silvia's
Popular disco in the resort centre.
✉ **Rua São Gonçalo de Lagos 3**

Cascais

Coconuts
The hottest disco on the Lisbon coast, full of energetic Lisboetas and foreign tourists.
✉ **Hotel Nau, Rua Dra Irancy Doyle**

Coimbra

States
Coimbra's trendiest nightspot, especially crowded on Friday and Saturday night during term time.
✉ **Praça Machado de Assis 22A** 🕐 **Open till 4AM, closed Sun**

Via Latina
A noisy nightclub which plays techno music.
✉ **Rua Almeida Garrett 1**
🕐 **Open till 4AM**

Faro

Barracuda
An open air disco, down on Faro beach.
🕐 **Open till 4AM**

Lagos

Inoxidável
A disco playing different sorts of music on different nights.
✉ **Rua Vasco da Gama 37**
🕐 **Open till 6AM**

Phoenix
A long-established nightclub, whose appeal never seems to wane. Always keeps up to date with contemporary music.
✉ **Rua 5 de Outubro**

Lisbon

Absoluto
Disco and occasional live bands.
✉ **Rua Dom Luis 1,** 🕐 **Open till 4AM. Closed Sun–Tue**

Café Central
Loud rock and a giant video screen.
✉ **Avenida 24 de Junho 112**
🕐 **Open till 4AM**

Décibel
Hard rock venue.
✉ **Avenida 24 de Junho 90B**
🕐 **Open till 3:30AM**

Frágil
A long-established but still very popular nightclub set in the heart of the Bairo Alto.
✉ **Rua da Atalaia 126–8**

Jamaica
Reggae and 1960s numbers for older rockers.
✉ **Rua Nova do Carvalho 6**

Kapital
Ultra-trendy, somewhat cliquéy. Mainly techno music downstairs, more middle-of-the-road on the other two floors.
✉ **Avenida 24 de Junho 68**
🕐 **Open till 5AM**

Kremlin
The latest of late-night venues attracting the fashionable young things of the city.
✉ **Escadinhas da Praia 5**
🕐 **Open till 7AM. Closed Sun, Mon and Wed**

Metalúrgica
A relaxed and popular nightclub, playing a variety of music.
✉ **Avenida 24 de Junho 110**
🕐 **Open till 4AM**

Plateau
Long established nightclub, which still has many devotees.
✉ **Escadinhas da Praia 3–7**
🕐 **Open till 6AM. Closed Sun and Mon**

Shangri-La
Tame-ish disco. 1970s and '80s rock.
✉ **Rua Nova do Carvalho 49–51**

Porto
Industria
A hugely popular nightclub set on the Foz do Douro water front.
✉ **Avenida do Brazil 843**

Rocks
Swinging bar and disco, in an old port 'lodge'.
✉ **228 Rua Rei Ramiro, Vila Nova de Gaia** 🕿 **02 301208**

Swing
Throbbing nightclub where Porto's trendiest hang out.
✉ **Centro Comercial Brasilia, Rotunda da Boavista**
🕿 **02 6090019**

Terminal X
A large disco, often playing world music.
✉ **Avenida de Feiritas Pereira de Malo 449**

Casinos
Gambling in Portugal is tightly controlled by law and restricted to adults. Formal attire is usually required, and you may be asked to show your passport. Games include roulette, baccarat, black jack and bingo, and 'one-armed bandit' slot machines. Most of Portugal's casinos are in traditional holiday resorts such as Povoa de Varzim, on the Minho coast, where the Porto wealthy used to spend the summer season, and Estoril, long a fashionable resort. These have been joined by new establishments on the Algarve.

The North
Casino da Figueira
✉ **Rua bernadino Lopo 56**
🕿 **033 22041**

Casino da Póvoa
✉ **Avenida braga, Póvoa de Varim** 🕿 **052 615151**

Casino Solverde
✉ **85 Rua 19, Espinho**

Lisbon Coast
Casino Estoril
✉ **Estoril** 🕿 **01 468 4521**

The Algarve
Casino de Montegordo
✉ **Vila Real de Santo António** 🕿 **081 512224**

Casino da Rocha
✉ **Edificio Tarik, Praia da Rocha, Portimão** 🕿 **082 23141**

Casino da Vilamoura
✉ **Vilamoura, Loule** 🕿 **089 302996**

Night Owls
The Portuguese are night owls at the best of times, particularly the young. When it comes to nightclubs, many people take pride in the lateness of their arrival, which is often 2AM or later. Dawn is considered a good time to leave.

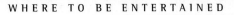

Theatre & *Fado*

Fado

Fado reached its greatest international phase during the 1950s, when the great *fadista* Amália Rodrigues toured the world and became, perhaps, the best known Portuguese of her generation. Her fame has waned, but she is still to be heard singing occasionally in top *fado* clubs.

Theatre

Lisbon

Teatro Nacional de Dona Maria II

Lisbon's principal theatre holds performances of Portuguese and foreign plays throughout the year except summer. Note that all productions are in Portuguese.

⊠ Rossio Square ☎ 01 422210

Teatro National de São Carlos

Stages opera and ballet productions and classical music concerts.

⊠ Largo São Carlos
☎ 01 346 5914

Teatro Municipal de São Luis

Another grand, old-fashioned theatre where Portuguese and international companies perform.

⊠ Rua António Maria Cardoso 40 ☎ 01 3427172

Fado

Coimbra

Diligencia

A bar where *fado* is often performed, particularly during the summer academic term.

⊠ Rua Nova 30 ☎ 039 27667

Lagos

O Muralho

Very touristy. *Fado* is not indigenous to the Algarve, but this is the best place to hear it.

⊠ Rua Infante de Sagres

Lisbon

All *fado* houses serve food and levy a cover charge. You can also come just to drink and listen to the music. The majority of venues can be found in the Bairro Alto district, and stay open until around 3AM.

A Severa

One of Lisbon's best known *fado* clubs, where many of Portugal's top *fadistas* perform.

⊠ Rua das Gáveas, 55
☎ 01 3464006

Lisboa a Noite

One of the more touristy places in the city. The owner herself performs with aplomb.

⊠ Rua das Gáveas 69
☎ 01 3468557

Parreirinha d'Alfama

Best of just a few *fado* houses based in the Alfama district.

⊠ Beco do Espirito Santo 1
☎ 01 8868209

Senhor Vinho

Top-notch, genuine *fado* performances, at reasonable prices.

⊠ Rua do Meio a Lapa 18
☎ 01 3972681
Ⓞ Closed Sun

Timpanas

Well away from the city centre, but this venue is well worth seeking out if you are eager to listen to the real McCoy.

⊠ Rua Gilberto 24, Alcântara
☎ 01 3972431 Ⓞ Closed Wed

Porto

Mal Cozinhado

A convivial restaurant which is set on the Ribeira, and which is also Porto's top *fado* venue.

⊠ Rua Outeirinho
☎ 02 2081319

Cinema

Faro
Cineclub de Faro
✉ 18 1 Dezembro
☎ 089 2 7627

Cinema Santo António
✉ 25 Santo António
☎ 089 823 308

Lagos
Cinema-Teatro Imperio
✉ Candido Reis
☎ 089 762 940

Lisbon
Amoreiras
A ten-screen cinema in the Amoreiras shopping complex.
✉ Avenida Duarte Pacheco
☎ 01 3831275

Cine Bolso
✉ Rua Actor Taborda 27B
☎ 01 3573407

Cine Camões
✉ Rua Loureto 15
☎ 01 3424194

Condes
✉ Avenida da Liberdade 2
☎ 01 342 2523

King Triplex
✉ Avenida Frei Miguel
Conteiras 52 ☎ 01 8480808

Londres
✉ Avenida Roma
☎ 01 8401313

Monumental
✉ Avenida Praia Vitória,
Edificio Monumental
☎ 01 3531859

Mundial
✉ Rua Martens Ferrão 12A
☎ 01 3538743

São Jorge
✉ Avenida da Liberdade 175
☎ 01 3579144

Tivoli
✉ Avenida da Liberdade 185
☎ 01 3141101

Portimão
Cine Esplanada
✉ Avenida 3, Praia da Rocha
☎ 082 703 332

Porto
Batalha
✉ Praça da Batalha
☎ 02 2022407

Casa das Artes
✉ Rua de António Cardoso 175
☎ 02 600 6153

Charlot
✉ Praça Mouzinho de
Albuquerque 113
☎ 02 609 8686

Estudio Foco
✉ Rua de Afonso Lopes
Vieira 54
☎ 02 609 3265

Lumiere
✉ Rua de José Falcão
☎ 02 208 1722

Passos Manuel
✉ Rua de Passos Manuel
☎ 02 200 5196

Pedro Cem
✉ Rua de Julio Dinis 103
☎ 02 609 0367

Sala Bébé
✉ Praça da Batalha
☎ 02 202 2407

Terço
✉ Rua João Pinto Ribeiro 680
☎ 02 581 966

Tavira
**Cine Teatro António
Pinheiro**
✉ Rua D Marcelino Franco
☎ 089 2 2671

Film Fans
Portuguese are enthusiastic cinema-goers. Foreign films are often released very soon after first showings in their native countries. They are virtually always shown in the original with Portuguese sub-titles.

What's On When

Precise dates vary from year to year.

February
Carnival weekend (which precedes Lent): festivities all over the country with streamers, fire-crackers, water-pistols and people in fancy dress. Particularly lively celebrations at Loulé in the Algarve, with processions through the streets and mock battles fought with fallen almond blossom.

March
Rally of Portugal: motor-racing rally through the north of the country (usually last week of the month).

Holy Week: processions and festivals take place all over Portugal during the week leading up to Easter. The greatest concentration of these is in the north. On Good Friday, crowds gather to do penance in Braga, religious capital of Portugal, in preparation for the Easter celebrations.

May
Festas das Cruzes (Feast of the Crosses) in Barcelos (first weekend): 16 crosses symbolising the Passion of Christ are erected to mark a procession route carpeted with flowers.

Fátima Day (13 May): this is the anniversary of the first apparition of the Virgin Mary to three shepherd children at Fátima in 1917.

June
Festa de São Gonçalo (the Feast of Saint Gonçalo) in Amarante (first weekend of the month).

Festas dos Santos Populares (Feasts of the People's Saints) in Lisbon (12–29 Jun). June is the capital's month of merrymaking, with the greatest festivities on the feast of Santo António on 12 and 13 Jun.

Porto's greatest festival, *São João* (St John), coincides with the summer solstice. Bonfires are lit and a huge firework display is staged (last week in Jun).

July/August
Festas da Rainha Santa (Festivals of the Holy Queen) in Coimbra. A week of cultural events (first week of Jul).

The National Handicrafts Fair in Vila do Conde, on the Minho coast (last week of Jul/first week of Aug).

Festas da Senhora da Agonia (Feast of Our Lady of Suffering). Otherwise known as simply the *Viana Festa*, this is one of the greatest and most popular festivals in Portugal (Fri–Sun nearest 29 Aug).

September
The wine harvest festival at Palmela, across the Tagus from Lisbon (second Sun in Sep).

Portuguese Grand Prix: motor-racing at Estoril (21 Sep).

November
National Gastronomic Fair in Santarém in the Ribatejo with samples of food and wine from all the different regions of Portugal (first week in Nov).

Practical Matters

GMT	Portugal	Germany	USA (NY)	Netherlands	Spain
12 noon	12 noon	1PM	7AM	1PM	1PM

BEFORE YOU GO

WHAT YOU NEED

- ● Required
- ○ Suggested
- ▲ Not required

	UK	Germany	USA	Netherlands	Spain
Passport/National Identity Card	●	●	●	●	●
Visa	▲	▲	▲	▲	▲
Onward or Return Ticket	▲	▲	▲	▲	▲
Health Inoculations	▲	▲	▲	▲	▲
Health Documentation (Reciprocal Agreement Document) ➤ 123, Health	●	●	▲	●	●
Travel Insurance	○	○	○	○	○
Driving Licence (national)	●	●	●	●	●
Car Insurance Certificate (if own car)	●	●	●	●	●
Car Registration Document (if own car)	●	●	●	●	●

WHEN TO GO

Portugal

▮▮▮ High season

▭ Low season

12°C	12°C	13°C	16°C	17°C	21°C	22°C	23°C	21°C	18°C	15°C	12°C
JAN	FEB	MAR	APR	MAY	JUN	JUL	AUG	SEP	OCT	NOV	DEC

🌧 Wet   ☁ Cloud   ☀ Sun   🌦 Sunshine & showers

TOURIST OFFICES

In the UK
Portuguese Trade and Tourism Office,
2nd Floor,
22–25A Sackville Street,
London W1X 1DE
☎ 0171 494 1441
Fax: 0171 494 1868

In the USA
Portuguese Trade and Tourism Office,
590 Fifth Avenue,
4th Floor,
New York
NY 10036–4704
☎ 212/354 4403
Fax: 212/764 6137

| POLICE 115 or 112 |
| AMBULANCE 115 or 112 |
| FIRE 115 or 112 |

WHEN YOU ARE THERE

ARRIVING

Portugal has three international airports – Lisbon, Porto and Faro. Scheduled and charter flights arrive daily at all of them from the UK and the rest of Europe, and there are direct flights to Lisbon, and charter flights to Porto, from North America.

Lisbon (Portela de Sacavem) Airport
Kilometres to city centre   Journey times

🚆	N/A
7 kilometres 🚌	30 minutes
🚗	15 minutes

Faro Airport
Kilometres to city centre   Journey times

🚆	N/A
4 kilometres 🚌	15 minutes
🚗	10 minutes

MONEY

The Portuguese unit of currency is the escudo (Esc), divided into 100 centavos (now rarely used). Its symbol, placed between the escudos and centavos, is the dollar sign ($). There are coins for 1, 5 and 10 escudos (all bronze) and 2.5, 20, 50, 100 and 200 escudos (all nickel); and banknotes for 500, 1,000, 2,000, 5,000 and 10,000 escudos. Escudos are known in slang as 'paus' (sticks). The 1,000 escudos is commonly, and since recently also officially, known as a 'conto'.

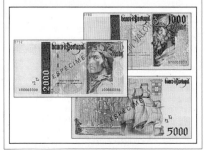

TIME

🕐 Portuguese time is the same as Greenwich Mean Time. The clocks are advanced one hour in spring, and brought back one hour in autumn. Continental Europe is always one hour ahead.

CUSTOMS

➔ **YES**

Goods Obtained Duty Free Inside the EU or Goods Bought Outside the EU (Limits):
Alcohol (over 22° vol) : 1L or
Alcohol (not over 22° vol): 2L and Still table wine: 2L
Cigarettes: 200 or Cigarillos: 100 or Cigars: 50 or Tobacco: 250gms
Perfume: 60cc
Toilet water: 250cc
Goods Obtained Duty and Tax Paid Inside the EU (Guidance Levels):
Alcohol (over 22° vol) : 10L
Alcohol (not over 22° vol): 20L
Wine (max 60L sparkling): 90L
Beer: 110L
Cigarettes: 800
Cigarillos: 400
Cigars: 200
Tobacco: 1kg
Perfume and Toilet Water: no limit
You must be 17 and over to benefit from the alcohol and tobacco allowances.

➖ **NO**

Drugs, firearms, ammunition, offensive weapons, obscene material, unlicensed animals.

TOURIST OFFICES

Costa de Lisboa
- Comissão Municipal de Turismo de Lisboa, Avenida 5 de Outubro 293, 1050 Lisboa (Lisbon)
  ☎ 01 793 4702
  Fax: 01 793 4628

Costa de Prata
- Região de Turismo do Centro, Largo da Portagem, 3000 Coimbra
  ☎ 039 33019
  Fax: 039 25576

Costa Verde
- Comissão Municipal de Turismo do Porto, Rua Clube dos Fenianos 25, 4000 Oporto (Porto)
  ☎ 02 323303
  Fax: 02 208 4548

Montanhas
- Região de Turismo de Dão Lafões, Avenida Gulbenkian, 3510 Viseu
  ☎ 032 422014
  Fax: 032 421864

Planícies
- Região de Turismo de Évora, Rua de Aviz 90, 7000 Évora ☎ 066 742534/5
  Fax: 066 25238

Algarve
- Região de Turismo do Algarve, Avenida 5 de Outubro 18, 8000 Faro
  ☎ 089 800400
  Fax: 089 800489

(See individual entries in towns for addresses and phone numbers of other tourist offices in Portugal.)

NATIONAL HOLIDAYS

J	F	M	A	M	J	J	A	S	O	N	D
1	1	2	2	2	2		1		1	1	4

1 Jan	New Year's Day
Feb/Mar	Shrove Tuesday
Mar/Apr	Good Friday
25 Apr	Liberty Day
1 May	Labour Day
May/Jun	Corpus Christi
10 Jun	Portugal Day
15 Aug	Feast of the Assumption
5 Oct	Republic Day
1 Nov	All Saints' Day
1 Dec	Independence Day
8 Dec	Feast of the Immaculate Conception
24 Dec	Christmas Eve
25 Dec	Christmas Day

OPENING HOURS

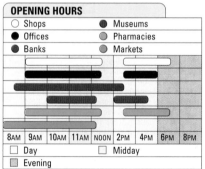

○ Shops   ● Museums
● Offices   ◐ Pharmacies
● Banks   ◐ Markets

| 8AM | 9AM | 10AM | 11AM | NOON | 2PM | 4PM | 6PM | 8PM |

☐ Day   ☐ Midday
▨ Evening

In addition to the times in the chart above, most shops close at 1PM on Saturday and are closed Sundays. In shopping centres located in cities and larger towns shops are open 10AM up to 11PM Monday to Saturday, sometimes Sunday as well. In tourist resorts and cities some supermarkets are open until 9PM. Hypermarkets are open 10AM to 11PM. As for pharmacies, each area has a pharmacy open until midnight, the location of which is advertised on pharmacy doors.
Most museums stick roughly to the opening times in the chart but many close Monday while some places also close Wednesday.

DRIVE ON THE RIGHT

TOILETS CHARGE

★★
★☆

PUBLIC TRANSPORT

 Internal Flights TAP Air Portugal ☎ 01 386 4080 and Portugália ☎ 01 842 5500 connect Lisbon, Porto and Faro. Portugália operates a *Ponte Areo* (Air Bridge) commuter service between Lisbon and Porto/Faro; no advance booking is needed, just turn up. Charter flights are also available.

 Trains The national railway company, Caminhos de Ferre Portugueses (CP) ☎ 01 346 5022, runs three types of service: *Regional* (stopping at most stations); *Intercidade* (stopping at only a few large towns); and *Rapido* (express train between Lisbon and Porto). Fares are reasonable with many discount schemes.

 Long Distance Buses The state-owned Rodoviária Nacional (RN) company (Lisbon ☎ 01 354 5775) covers most of the country, much more extensively than the rail network. Long distance buses (*RN Expressos*) are mostly comfortable. There are several private companies also operating an extensive service.

 Ferries From Lisbon, ferries cross the Rio Tejo to the suburb of Cacilhas every 10 to 15 minutes (from 7AM to 9PM) from Fluvial terminal, adjacent to Praça do Comércio, or Cais de Sodré (24-hour service), taking 15 minutes. From Setúbal there is a 24-hour service across to the Tróia Peninsula, at least hourly, journey 20 minutes.

 Urban Transport In the main towns there is a complete public transport network. In Lisbon the state-owned Carris company runs buses, the underground (*Metropolitano*), quaint electric trams (*eléctricos*), and funiculars and lifts (both called *elevadores*). Useful guide: *Guia Informativo de Carris.*

CAR RENTAL

Prices are relatively cheap. You will find the major international companies in Lisbon, Porto and the Algarve. If using one of the many local firms offering competitive rates, check the vehicle is in good condition and that adequate insurance is included.

TAXIS

 These are cream in colour, and are good value by western European standards. In towns meters are used; it is worth checking that they are switched on. Outside urban areas the charge is per kilometre. Between 10PM and 6AM the rate increases by 20 per cent.

DRIVING

 Speed limit on motorways (*autoestradas*): **120kph**; minimum: **40kph**

 Speed limit on dual carriageways: **100kph**; country roads: **90kph**

 Speed limits on urban roads: **50kph**

 Seat Belts must be worn in front seats at all times and in rear seats where fitted.

 Breath Testing: random tests are carried out.

Fuel (*gasolina*) is available in three grades: super (98 octane), *sem chumbo* (unleaded 95 octane), and *super sem chumbo* (unleaded 98 octane). Prices are the same everywhere. Filling stations are open 8AM to midnight (some 24 hours). The carrying of petrol in cans in cars is forbidden.

 Orange SOS telephones are located at regular intervals along motorways and other main roads. A breakdown service is operated by the national motoring organisation, the Automóvel Club de Portugal (ACP). For assistance, ☎ 01 942 5095 in the south and ☎ 02 830 1127 in the north. Place a red warning triangle 30m behind your vehicle.

PERSONAL SAFETY

Theft from cars and other petty crime is increasingly a problem, especially in the Algarve. Car stereos are particularly at risk. The Polícia de Segurança Pública are the urban police to whom any crime should be reported; in tourist areas, some wear red armbands with CD on them. Remember:

- Never leave anything of value in your car.
- Do not leave valuables on the beach or poolside.
- Leave valuables in hotel safe deposit boxes.
- Don't walk alone through dimly lit areas at night.

Police assistance:
☎ **115 or 112**
from any call box

TELEPHONES

Public telephones on the street and in many cafés and bars accept 10, 20 and 50 escudos coins, while others can only be used with phone cards. Calls can also be made from post offices where you pay the operator on completion of the call. The cost is a little more than dialling from a call box but is a lot cheaper than calling from your hotel room.

International Dialling Codes

From Portugal to:

UK:	00 44
Germany:	00 49
USA:	00 1
Netherlands:	00 31
Spain:	00 34

POST

Post Offices
There is at least one *correio* (post office) in every town and reasonably large village. They sell stamps as do many places with *correios* signs. In small towns they close for lunch, otherwise hours are:
Open: 8:30AM–6PM
Closed: Sat and Sun

ELECTRICITY

The native power supply is: 220 volts

Sockets take two-round-pin continental-style plugs. Visitors from the UK require an adaptor and US visitors a voltage transformer.

TIPS/GRATUITIES

Yes ✓ No ✗		
Restaurants (if service not included)	✓	10%
Cafés/bars	✓	10%
Taxis	✓	10%
Tour guides	✓	200$
Porters	✓	100–200$
Chambermaids	✓	500$
Cloakroom attendants	✓	100$
Hairdressers	✓	200$
Theatre/cinema usherettes	✓	100$
Toilets	✓	100$

What to photograph: the shimmering Costa de Prata (Silver Coast), colourful fishing ports, ancient villages, hilltop castles and the rugged mountains of the north east.

Restrictions: do not take photographs at airports, military bases, military docks or anywhere your action could be construed as breaching security.

Buying film: all popular brands and types of film and camera batteries are readily available and are reasonably priced.

HEALTH

Insurance
Nationals of EU and certain other countries receive free emergency medical treatment in Portugal with the relevant documentation (Form E111 for UK nationals), although private medical insurance is still advised and is essential for all other visitors.

Dental Services
Dental treatment for EU nationals is very limited under the state scheme. You will probably have to pay and the charges are not refundable; other visitors will certainly have to pay. Private medical insurance will cover you.

Sun Advice
Sunburn and sunstroke are common problems in summer (especially during July and August), particularly in the south of the country. Do not be deceived by a cooling wind off the Atlantic. Avoid prolonged exposure and use a sunscreen or cover up.

Drugs
Prescription and non-prescription drugs and medicines are available from pharmacies (*fármacias*), distinguished by a large green cross. Chemists, who are trained in basic health care, will prescribe remedies for minor ailments.

Safe Water
Tap water is generally safe but not too pleasant. Anywhere, but especially outside the main cities, towns and resorts, it is advisable to drink bottled water (*água mineral*), either *sem gás* (still) or *com gás* (carbonated).

CONCESSIONS

Students/Youths The International Student Identity Card (ISIC) for students, and the International Youth Card (IYC) for those under 26, entitles holders to discounts on transport and fees for museums and attractions. The Cartão Jovem (youth card), for those between 12 and 26, gives a 50 per cent discount on rail journeys over 50km.

Senior Citizens Winter holidays in the Algarve are popular with older travellers. Low-cost, flight-only deals are available from some countries, and you can find long-term accommodation for a fraction of the high-season rate. Over 65s (on proof of age) receive a 50 per cent reduction on all suburban trains, except weekdays between 6:30–9:30AM and 5–8PM.

CLOTHING SIZES

Portugal	UK	Rest of Europe	USA	
46	36	46	36	Suits
48	38	48	38	
50	40	50	40	
52	42	52	42	
54	44	54	44	
56	46	56	46	
41	7	41	8	Shoes
42	7.5	42	8.5	
43	8.5	43	9.5	
44	9.5	44	10.5	
45	10.5	45	11.5	
46	11	46	12	
37	14.5	37	14.5	Shirts
38	15	38	15	
39/40	15.5	39/40	15.5	
41	16	41	16	
42	16.5	42	16.5	
43	17	43	17	
34	8	34	6	Dresses
36	10	36	8	
38	12	38	10	
40	14	40	12	
42	16	42	14	
44	18	44	16	
38	4.5	38	6	Shoes
38	5	38	6.5	
39	5.5	39	7	
39	6	39	7.5	
40	6.5	40	8	
41	7	41	8.5	

- Remember to contact the airport on the day prior to leaving to ensure the flight details are unchanged.
- You must report to the departure terminal of the airport not later than the time indicated on your ticket and/or the published timetables.
- You must comply with the import regulations of the country you are travelling to (check before departure).

LANGUAGE

The native language is Portuguese, a Latin language like French, Italian and Spanish. A knowledge of Spanish and/or French makes Portuguese easy to read, however, speaking it is somewhat trickier. Despite obvious similarities between Spanish and Portuguese spelling, Portuguese words sound very different from their ostensible Spanish equivalents. Even so, almost all Portuguese understand Spanish and in the tourist areas English is widely spoken. However, knowing a few Portuguese words will make your trip more rewarding. Below is a list of some words that might be useful. More extensive coverage can be found in the AA's *Essential Portuguese Phrase Book* which lists over 2,000 phrases and 2,000 words.

hotel	*hotel*	breakfast	*pequeno almoço*
room	*quarto*	toilet	*banho*
...single/double	*simples/de casal*	bath	*banheira*
...one/two nights	*livre*	shower	*duche*
...per person/per room	*um/doi noite(s)*	balcony	*varanda*
	por pessoa/por quarto	key	*chave*
		room service	*serviço de quarto*
reservation	*reserva*	chambermaid	*camareira*
rate	*preço*	television	*televisão*

bank	*banco*	American dollar	*dólare americano*
exchange office	*casa de câmbio*	exchange rate	*câmbio*
post office	*correio*	bank card	*cartão do banco*
counter	*guiché*	credit card	*cartão de crédito*
money	*dinheiro*	giro bank card	*cartão dos correios*
small change	*dinheiro trocado*	cheque	*cheque*
foreign currency	*moeda estrangeira*	traveller's cheque	*traveller cheque*
pound sterling	*libra esterlina*	giro cheque	*cheque de correio*

restaurant	*restaurante*	starter	*entrada*
bar/café	*café*	dish	*prato*
table	*mesa*	main course	*prato principal*
menu	*ementa*	dish of the day	*prato do dia*
tourist menu	*ementa turística*	dessert	*sobremesa*
wine list	*lista de vinhos*	drink	*bebida*
lunch	*almoço*	waiter	*garçom/empregado*
dinner	*jantar*	bill	*conta*

aeroplane	*avião*	bus	*autocarro*
airport	*aeroporto*	..station	*estação de*
flight	*vôo*		*camionetas*
train	*comboio*	..stop	*paragem de*
..station	*estação caminho de ferro*		*autocarro*
		ferry	*barco*
ticket	*bilhete*	..port	*estação marítima*
..single/return	*ida/ida e volta*	timetable	*horário*
..first/second class	*primeira/segunda classe*	seat	*lugar*
		non-smoking	*não funadores*

yes	*sim*	help!	*ajuda!*
no	*não*	today	*hoje*
please	*se faz favor*	tomorrow	*amanhã*
thank you	*obrigado*	yesterday	*ontem*
hello	*óla*	how much?	*quanto?*
goodbye	*adeus*	open	*aberto*
excuse me!	*desculpe!*	closed	*fechado*

INDEX

Acknowledgements
The Automobile Association wishes to thank the following libraries, photographers and associations for their assistance in the preparation of this book:

IMAGES COLOUR LIBRARY cover (c): fishing boat
MARY EVANS PICTURE LIBRARY 10a, 11, 14
MRI BANKERS' GUIDE TO FOREIGN CURRENCY 119
PICTURES COLOUR LIBRARY cover (a): Albufeira, 31
SPECTRUM COLOUR LIBRARY 47
ZEFA PICTURES LTD 26

The remaining pictures are from the Association's own library (AA PHOTO LIBRARY) and were taken by:
M BIRKETT 9b, 19, 48, 51, 63b, 73, 75, 80, 83, 86, 87, 90; J EDMANSON 8b, 25, 62, 67, 68b, 71, 74, 76, 77b, 81, 82, 91a, 117b; A KOUPRIANOFF cover (b): ceramic, back cover: tomatoes, 2, 5a, 5b, 6, 7, 8a, 9b, 10b, 12, 13, 15a, 18, 20, 21, 22, 24, 27a, 27b, 32/3, 34, 35, 36, 37b, 39, 40, 41, 43b, 44, 49, 53, 54, 55a, 56, 57, 58, 63a, 64b, 65, 66, 68a, 69, 77a, 78, 79, 84, 85, 81b, 122c; J A TIMS 60; P WILSON 1, 16, 17, 23, 29, 37a, 38, 43a, 45, 46, 50, 55b, 59, 61, 64a, 70, 72, 117a, 122a, 122b

Contributors
Copy editor: Hilary Hughes Page Layout: Design 23 Verifier: Emma Rowley Ruas
Researcher (Practical Matters): Colin Follett Indexer: Marie Lorimer

Essential
Portugal

by Martin Symington

PASSPORT BOOKS
NTC/Contemporary Publishing Group

Published by Passport Books, a division of NTC/
Contemporary Publishing Group, Inc. 4255 West
Touhy Avenue, Lincolnwood (Chicago), Illinois
60646–1975 U.S.A.

Above: *football scarves*

Page 1: *Pinhão station*

Page 5a: *fishing boats,
Tavira*

Page 15a: *Mosteiro dos
Jerónimos*
Page 15b: *jewelry, Museu
Calouste Gulbenkian*

Page 27b: *azulejo tiles*

Page 48: *Campo de Santa
Clara, Lisbon*

Page 66: *Portalegre*

Page 80: *Praia da Rocha*

Page 91b: *statue of São
Vicente*

Page 117a: *cockerels,
Barcelos market*

The contents of this publication are believed correct at
the time of printing. Nevertheless, the publishers cannot
accept responsibility for errors or omissions, nor for
changes in details given. We are always grateful to
readers who let us know of any errors or omissions
they come across, and future printings will be updated
accordingly.

Published by Passport Books in conjunction with
The Automobile Association of Great Britain.

Written by Martin Symington

Library of Congress Catalog Card Number: 98-65041
ISBN 0–8442–0125–1

Color separation: BTB Digital Imaging, Whitchurch,
Hampshire

Printed and bound in Italy by Printer Trento srl

The weather chart on **page 118** of this book is
calibrated in °C. For conversion to °F simply use the
following formula:
$$°F = 1.8 × °C + 32$$